W9-BHY-880

The Anger HABIT™ in PARENTING

A New Approach to Understanding and Resolving Family Conflict

Carl Semmelroth, PhD

SOURCEBOOKS, INC.®
NAPERVILLE, ILLINOIS

This publication is designed to provide accurate and authoritative information in regard to the subject matter covered. It is sold with the understanding that the publisher is not engaged in rendering legal, accounting, or other professional service. If legal advice or other expert assistance is required, the services of a competent professional person should be sought.—*From a Declaration of Principles Jointly Adopted by a Committee of the American Bar Association and a Committee of Publishers and Associations*

All brand names and product names used in this book are trademarks, registered trademarks, or trade names of their respective holders. Sourcebooks, Inc., is not associated with any product or vendor in this book.

This book is not intended as a substitute for medical advice from a qualified physician. The intent of this book is to provide accurate general information in regard to the subject matter covered. If medical advice or other expert help is needed, the services of an appropriate medical professional should be sought.

Published by Sourcebooks, Inc.
P.O. Box 4410, Naperville, Illinois 60567-4410
(630) 961-3900
FAX: (630) 961-2168
www.sourcebooks.com

Library of Congress Cataloging-in-Publication Data

Semmelroth, Carl.
   The anger habit in parenting : a new approach to understanding and resolving family conflict / by Carl Semmelroth, PhD.
      p. cm.
   Includes index.
   ISBN 1-4022-0336-5 (alk. paper)
   1. Anger. 2. Child rearing. 3. Habit breaking. I. Title.

BF575.A5S455 2005
649'.1--dc22

2005003051

Printed and bound in the United States of America.
VP 10 9 8 7 6 5 4 3 2 1

To Judith M. Smith and Donald E. P. Smith
whose 1964 work, *Child Management:
A Program for Parents and Teachers,*
led the way for disciplined child management
without anger and threats.

Table of Contents

Acknowledgments

Forty years have passed since the publication of Smith and Smith's book *Child Management: A Program for Parents and Teachers*. Those exciting days in Ann Arbor, Michigan, with uncountable numbers of discussions with Don Smith about child management, child development, and the foundations of behavior change continue to be a reference point for me and greatly influenced this book.

My wife, Sara Semmelroth, has been my partner for forty-six years, as a mother of our five children, as a partner in our private counseling practice, and always as an initiator for trying new things. Helping others is as instinctual for her as breathing. As with previous books, she was the first person to read the original draft of each chapter as it was written, and her comments and reactions were my initial signals as to whether I was on track or had lost my way.

Our daughters, Melissa and Jean, also watched over the book as it came into being. Melissa is my self-appointed private cheerleader. She is always there with encouragement and believes in me with superhuman tenacity. Jean applies her brilliant, but patient, question asking to each chapter as it is written and provides examples from her own family experience. Jean and Steve's daughter, our seven-year-old granddaughter, Kathy, is the exemplar of those children who will never submit to another person's will.

Louise Waller, my editor, continues to apply her magical power to my writings, which, like a philosopher's stone, transforms them into books. I continue to receive, entirely undeservedly, the benefit of her skills that were honed in a career as psychology editor for several large publishing companies. I am grateful.

Introduction
How to Get the Most Out of This Book

The book is meant for use by individuals, groups, and workshops concerned with child management and anger. Because the chapters each stand on their own, therapists, group leaders, and individual readers can feel free to study them in the order that meets their needs.

Individuals who are studying the book on their own are strongly encouraged to read chapter 1 first. It contains information about anger in general and a way of looking at how anger grows.

Most lessons contain exercises that will help you understand and change your behaviors so that your family and children benefit. Each exercise starts with real-life examples that guide you and function as a model for carrying out the exercise. The more you work at these exercises, the more apt you will be to make rewarding changes in your family life. You will come to see anger as the drag that it is.

We strongly suggest that you keep a private notebook or journal while working through the book. At the end of most lessons are examples of how to record successes in making real-life changes. Recording positive changes will be a great help to you in sustaining your efforts and making a lasting difference in your life and in the lives of your children.

We all want the very best for our children and we want to be perfect parents for them. Your tendency may be to condemn yourself as a bad parent when you lose it or otherwise fall short of your ideal. Please be gentle and understanding with yourself as you try to make real changes suggested here. None of us are perfect. Small steps in the right direction start us on any long journey. Even two steps forward and one step back results in progress. Use the material here as a map that you can consult in finding the direction you wish to travel, and take the first steps. Getting even partway there will result in meaningful differences for you and your family. Bon voyage.

Chapter 1
The Anger Chain

Angela's arm freezes as she starts to hit her four-year-old son. The look on his face defuses her rage in mid-detonation. That place behind her eyes instantly throbs as his expression is imprinted there like a red-hot brand on the front of her brain. Instantly she knows it will always be there. Eddie's eyes, big as saucers, broadcast his recognition of a horror he has never before experienced—he feels unsafe with his mother.

Electrifying shame replaces Angela's exhaustion, produced by her screaming tirade. Eddie moves away from her as she tries to hold him in a "first-aid" attempt to keep her dreams alive for both of them.

The last vestige of her confidence as a parent is replaced by self-hatred and depression. Her dreams of being the mother she wished her mother had been, of love and being loved, of good times recorded in pictures that she would treasure forever, these seem like a terrible joke. Things haven't gone that way at all.

Her irritations with Eddie's eating and sleeping "problems" as an infant turned into disgust during his toilet training. She never thought

> she would resort to shaming and mocking her own child. Her impatience with the endless repetition of his two-year-old "no" turned into yelling. Raising her voice at him when he wouldn't mind her turned into shouting and threatening. And now this.
>
> "I'm a horrible mother and a horrible person," she thinks. "I was so stupid to think I should ever have been a parent. It was just a dream. I hate this and I hate myself. I never realized I'm such an angry, awful person."
>
> Angela is quite capable of being a very good parent and providing a healthy, safe, and disciplined home for her child. The problem isn't that Angela doesn't know that she is an "angry, awful person." She isn't. The problem is that Angela doesn't know much about anger. In particular, she doesn't know what makes her anger grow and what to do about it.

Anger is about control. Many parents are caught up in attempts to control their children and in doing so, fill their households with angry interactions. As this happens, the parents become more frustrated and miserable, while the children become more distant and often out of control.

It is helpful to understand how and why anger, once planted in the family, tends to grow in frequency and intensity. Like an addictive drug, more extreme anger is required and it is required more often in order to satisfy the anger habit.

First, a distinction about anger terms:

1. Others do not see our angry thoughts and feelings, so we will call these internal events *preparation for angry behaviors.* Among these are feelings of irritation, being offended, being victimized, planning for revenge, thinking of others' imperfections, and feelings of righteous indignation.

2. Our angry actions and displays can be seen by other people so they are called *angry behaviors*. Among these are angry facial expressions, angry words, threatening gestures, hitting, and even killing.

The important point here is that: angry feelings and thoughts (#1) prepare us to carry out angry behaviors (#2).

When a father reacts to his son's sloppy lawn mowing with a feeling of anger, the father's body is preparing for a physical attack on his son. The angry feeling is literally his sensing, his physical awareness, of these internal body preparations. Chemicals have been released in his body that are busy speeding up his heart, providing more blood flow to his arms and legs, and increasing his blood pressure. These physical changes are tuning up the father's body for a physical attack on his son.

You will find it shocking to think of your feeling of anger in such raw terms. We are ordinarily unaware that our feeling of anger is our body's preparation for physically attacking someone. We hardly ever carry through with a physical attack. Usually our exhibited angry behaviors warn the other person that we are preparing to attack them. That warning, taken with some degree of seriousness, is often enough to get us what we want. Our facial expressions may be enough to make a child turn down the stereo. If that is not enough, speaking in an angry way may work. And if that does not do it, we may shout at the child in a threatening manner.

Regardless of how well we paint over our parenting anger as being needed and natural, the possible effectiveness of any of these angry behaviors depends on them being experienced by children as steps toward physical harm. That is, the effectiveness of angry behaviors depends on children learning to avoid what might follow. Effective parental anger must cause children to experience fear.

Angry feelings and angry behaviors are connected, forming a chain that stretches from mild irritation with an accompanying facial grimace, to a feeling of rage accompanied by an all-out physical attack. Once parents start using anger to manage their children, their angry thoughts and behaviors tend to move toward the extreme end of the anger chain.

Consider these interactions between parent and child:

- Ten-month-old Celia crawls under a living room table and pulls out the telephone charging transformer from the wall plug.
- Celia's father, Jack, interrupts his TV watching and gets down on his hands and knees to retrieve Celia and replace the transformer. He picks her up, places her in front of his chair, and puts several toys around her.
- Celia promptly crawls toward the table again. Jack barely catches up to her before she gets under the table. He picks her up and says, "You little dickens. You cannot do that. Come over here and play with your blocks."
- When she is released, Celia again heads straight for the table. Jack says, "No, Celia. You can't do that." Celia stops and looks at her father. She laughs. He smiles at her. She then proceeds under the table and gets to the transformer before Jack pulls her out. She cries. Her father gets more serious and says, "You can't do that," in a loud voice. He takes her back to his chair and sits her by her blocks.
- Celia picks up a block, and then drops it and heads at full speed toward the table. Jack yells, "No!" He starts to get up. Celia stops, looks at him, and moves on. Jack rushes over

while shouting, "No." He grabs her roughly and puts her in her crib where she cries herself to sleep.

Three years later, when Celia is four, Jack takes her with him shopping at the grocery store.

- Celia says, "I want to go home." Her father says, "This will only take a few minutes and I don't want to listen to you whine the whole time." He places her in the grocery cart.
- Celia reaches out and pulls at a can on the grocery shelf. In an angry voice Jack says, "Stop that!"
- Celia reaches out again when they are in the next aisle and pulls a box of breakfast cereal off the shelf. Jack yells, "You stop that! You wait until we get home and see what you get if you don't cut it out!"
- Celia grabs a package of gum in the checkout line. Her father retrieves it and slaps her.

Jack has regressed along the anger chain from mildly angry interventions with Celia to slapping and hitting her three years later. Any thought or feeling along the right side of the table below carries with it the tendency to go further along the anger chain.

The Anger Chain

Some Angry Feelings Lead To… The Anger Chain, Which Leads To… Some Angry Behaviors

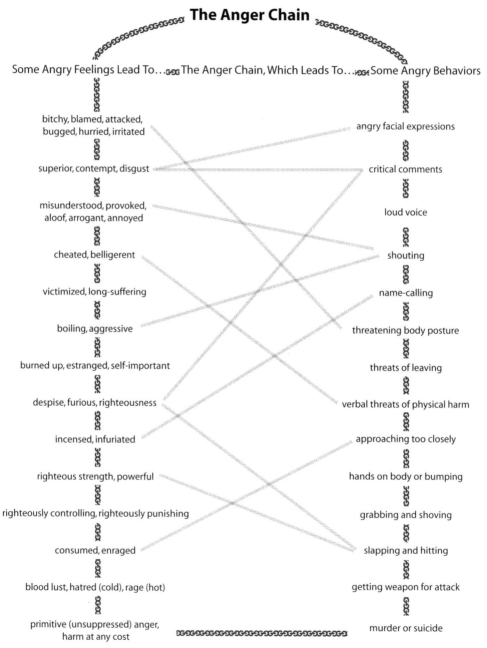

bitchy, blamed, attacked, bugged, hurried, irritated

angry facial expressions

superior, contempt, disgust

critical comments

misunderstood, provoked, aloof, arrogant, annoyed

loud voice

cheated, belligerent

shouting

victimized, long-suffering

name-calling

boiling, aggressive

threatening body posture

burned up, estranged, self-important

threats of leaving

despise, furious, righteousness

verbal threats of physical harm

incensed, infuriated

approaching too closely

righteous strength, powerful

hands on body or bumping

righteously controlling, righteously punishing

grabbing and shoving

consumed, enraged

slapping and hitting

blood lust, hatred (cold), rage (hot)

getting weapon for attack

primitive (unsuppressed) anger, harm at any cost

murder or suicide

For example, the feeling of irritation with your children carries with it the tendency to go beyond angry facial expressions and to engage in critical comments. Likewise, feelings of self-importance carry with them the tendency to go beyond threatening to leave the family or withhold money or withhold love. They also tend to carry you into feelings of righteous power and corresponding physical threats.

> **Anger carries with it the tendency to go down the anger chain toward destructive behaviors.**

Many families, like Jack and his daughter, tend to increase anger reactions over many years. When Celia was born, Jack could not have imagined ever slapping her. Now that she is four, he cannot imagine ever becoming murderously angry with her. But the "natural" path of anger is to become more extreme with use. Jack did not understand that when he began using threats regularly with his young child, he was setting himself up for getting increasingly angry over the years.

The anger chain also applies to other anger experiences. Jack's reaction to drivers who cut him off, his wife's overspending, and many things in his life that don't go the way he would like are apt to deteriorate according to his own characteristic version of the anger chain.

> **Frustrating situations produce escalation in anger along the anger chain. Individuals have their own unique anger chains.**

Some people have a very compact anger chain. When things do not go the way they want or expect, they start with shouting and immediately resort to physical attack. Most people think that these people are the only ones who have an anger problem. This is like saying that only people who drink alcohol until they are in a coma every day have an alcohol problem.

The way a person's anger escalates in a situation that does not go well for them is the way their anger will escalate over years as a parent. For example, suppose you had a tendency to feel self-important when you were younger. As a result, you sometimes got into confrontations with others who did not respond to your demands. Then you had a family. You are likely to threaten to leave your family later in life when they don't respond to your demands. When that doesn't work, you are likely to respond with righteous fury along with using verbal and physical threats. Self-importance makes other people pay for their non-deference.

Exercise 1-A: What Is My Anger Chain Like?

Using the anger chain as a guide, try to remember your feelings and actions on two occasions you became very angry outside of your role as a parent. Where did you start out on the chain? Where did you end up? You need not spend a lot of time trying to diagnose your anger. The remainder of the book will take you through an examination of the characteristic patterns of parental anger. The goal here is to recognize that your angry feelings and your behaviors have some patterns.

An example will help you see how to figure out your anger chain.

Example: Describe a Major Anger Incident

My wife and I got into it big-time a while ago. All I did was to ask her if she had gotten the oil changed in her car lately. She ignored me and I asked again in a louder voice. Soon we were shouting. I finally said I was getting tired of living with a nitwit.

She slammed the dish she was carrying on the kitchen table and left the room. I was feeling as if I had not done anything and she just did not appreciate that I try to take care of things. I got madder and madder the more I thought about it. I imagined getting in her face and telling her a thing or two.

Where Does This Incident Put You on the Anger Chain?

Well she is always accusing me of criticizing her. I guess that's the way she took my question about her car. When I look at "Critical Comments" on the anger chain and the corresponding feelings, I think I do feel superior to my wife about many things. When she doesn't take care of things the way I would, I guess I feel some contempt. I certainly went quickly down the Chain from there through "loud voice" and "shouting" to "name-calling." When she left the room, it was if I still had to go lower down the chain.

Your Example 1:

_____
_____
_____
_____
_____
_____

Describe a Major Anger Incident:

_____
_____
_____
_____
_____
_____

Where Does This Incident Put You on the Anger Chain?

_____

_____

_____

_____

_____

_____

Your Example 2:

_____

_____

_____

_____

_____

Describe a Major Anger Incident:

_____

_____

_____

_____

_____

Where Does This Incident Put You on the Anger Chain?

_____

_____

_____

_____

_____

Your angry behaviors and thoughts when you confront problems in your life as a whole are likely to set the pattern for your parenting anger. The difference is likely to be that you will be more extreme and go further down the anger chain in parenting than with adults. This is because people tend to feel they have a right to control their children and, because children are less powerful and less experienced with self-defense, they make easier targets than adults.

Several things can exaggerate anger. The anger chain is more quickly and easily descended when fear-reducing drugs such as alcohol are involved. Drugs that tend to affect thinking, such as amphetamines, can also give anger a boost. In addition, those mental illnesses that produce disorganized thinking take people quickly down the anger chain.

Finally, location can make a major difference. Anger sometimes explodes down the anger chain if a person feels they are on home ground and someone is seen as an invader. Police persons are rightfully concerned about entering the home of an angry person.

The most dangerous combination of factors relating to the anger chain is a person who:

- has a history of violence;
- takes mind-altering drugs;
- is intoxicated on alcohol;
- has a history of thought-disordered mental illness; and
- is at home with family present.

If you have a problem with anger, don't drink, don't take drugs, take your prescribed medication for mental illness, and stay away from your family if you are violating any of these.

Parental anger can only be cured by finding better ways to parent than to try to control children with threats. Much of this book is devoted to helping parents find alternatives to anger.

Parenting involves finding solutions to a long series of problems extending over many years. Children start out in life smaller than we are. They initially readily respond to us when we raise our voices or when we make mild threats. This makes it easy for parents to use anger to solve problems with children in the beginning. What begins as mild anger has a tendency to grow as has been illustrated in this chapter, to descend the anger chain. This book shows parents alternatives to anger as a way to solve the problems of parenting.

Anger easily becomes a habit, a habit that grows and becomes more destructive. The happiness and well-being of your children, your family, and yourself makes it important to examine the anger habit. Restoring the family setting to the safe place it is meant to be so children can grow and learn is worth more than a little effort.

Take your time with this book. Changing isn't easy. It never comes by just reading something. That is why there are exercises included in each chapter. Doing them will help you actually make changes in your everyday life.

Most chapters also have suggestions at the end for keeping a record of successful change. Behavior change is helped enormously by recording positive results. You are strongly urged to devote a private notebook to a record of your successes. If you work at it, you will have many successes to record.

Chapter 2
Making and Enforcing Rules

Susan's jaw clenches and her grip tightens on the steering wheel as she guides the spotless Envoy into her garage. She walks back onto the drive just to check if her impression was correct. Hands on hips, she surveys the uncut, five-inch grass lawn like a general surveying a battlefield at the end of a lost battle.

Thirteen-year-old John doesn't hear Susan's yell from downstairs over the noise of his stereo. His face takes on the disgusted look he usually reserves for his sister as he hears his mother's angry voice outside his door.

Five minutes later Susan feels just awful. John feels numb and alone. Susan's performance is over. John's stereo is broken; he can no longer play baseball; his allowance is stopped; and he feels his mother hates him.

Susan is in her room, carefully hanging up her expensive new suit. She tries in vain to make herself feel better by casting her thoughts back to a big commission she earned recently at work. She works to exhaustion every day and loves it. But how can she deal with John too? Her face hurts from crying and trying not to cry at the same time. "What will it take to make him obey the rules?" she asks herself. If only he would cooperate.

Our goal as parents is to nurture, protect, teach, and welcome the young into our culture. We all know that we cannot live together in a civilized manner without rules. We all know that children need rules. But what is a rule and what is its purpose in parenting?

Do we make rules to control children? If you think your job as a parent is to control your child, your use of rules will be an attempt to control them. Control requires being ready to punish, so consequently you will be ready to be angry. Control involves "making" someone do something, and sooner or later always comes down to having the biggest stick, the most powerful threat, and the willingness to use threats to engender fear.

Susan views rules as a way of making John do what she wants. John regularly breaks her rules. For example, "Mow the lawn every Friday before I get home." Susan gets more and more angry every time John breaks her rules. She regularly increases the intensity of his punishment. These punishments, made in anger, seem extreme, even to her after she calms down. She regularly backs down.

If you view rules as a way of controlling children, then you will make breaking rules more and more hurtful. And if children continue to break the rules, more hurt is demanded. Your theory of control requires that you set up a situation where alternatives to doing what you want children to do are so painful that they will choose to comply with your rules. For example, they sit and suffer boredom day after day in a do-nothing class at school rather than skipping school and then being grounded, hit, yelled at, or worse.

Susan doesn't really want to control John. She instinctively knows that successful control would require squashing his independence. Susan likes his independent attitude. But she knows no alternative to punishing John as an attempt to control him.

Susan's problem with John is common today. Many parents see the need for rules, but don't know how to administer the rules except by escalating hurtful consequences. Often consequences are "promised" in anger. Because they are too extreme for the parent to actually carry out, except in anger, they are *only* carried out in anger.

An alternative to using rules to control children is to use rules to influence children's control of themselves. This requires changing two things that Susan and most parents do:

- Consequences for breaking a rule must stay the same every time the rule is broken in order to influence children's self-control.
- The enforcement of rules must communicate to children their parent's unchanging expectations concerning children's behaviors. So, parents must be present when rules are broken in order to demonstrate those expectations by enforcing them.

We will leave the problem of being present until later in this chapter. Dealing with it usually involves painstaking examination of parent's economic and life-style priorities. For example, Susan likes nice things—expensive clothes, cars, house, and furnishings. She doesn't yet realize that the time required to earn enough to buy these things is not their only cost. Less time with John costs her influence on John's self-control.

Parents may believe that in order to be effective, rules must be consistently enforced. But they don't do it. What is missed is that in order to be consistent, the enforcement must be the same every time a rule is broken. The reason this is missed is that:

- If parents view rules as a way to control a child's behavior, then every time the rule is tested (broken), the parent thinks the rule is defective and throws it away. It didn't control the child.
- They are right. If rules are supposed to control behavior then breaking the rule means it didn't work. A stronger rule is needed—one with enforcements that hurt the child more.
- If the function of rules in parenting is not the parents' control of children, but children's control of themselves, consequences of rule infraction needs to be the same every time.
- Rules function to inform children of our unshakable expectations concerning their behavior, just as the laws of nature inform them how to behave by giving them consistent consequences. A wall always has the same effect when children bump into it. It doesn't control children; it influences them to control themselves. They use the door.

Inconsistency in enforcing rules undermines their aid to children's feeling of safety and their self-control, just as walls that sometimes let them through and sometimes don't would confuse and frighten them. Children do not automatically know what their future behaviors are going to be. If we believe that they will one day live and flourish in a civilized culture, we must inform children of our belief in their future. Rules help us do that if they are ironclad consistent. If they change, and so the consequences change, while we wallow all over the place when children misbehave, then rules are anything but definite expectations. As a result, rules are revealed as parental attempts to take control of the child's behavior.

As discussed in chapter 3, children will always struggle for control and the struggle can get very complicated. Even when the parent sees the child as a good "Dubie," and uses escalating punishment to enforce rules, the child is likely to have developed a secret life the parent knows nothing about. All of us need to feel in control of ourselves, even when we are children. There are many ways to maintain that sense of autonomy, some more perverse than others, even in the face of tyrannical parental practices.

When we get involved with rules as control mechanisms we cut ourselves off from our children's formation of self-determined behavior. Control, when successful, produces *involuntary behavior*. Communication is self-determined behavior and is therefore *voluntary*.

> **Rules, viewed as unshakable expectations, influence the child's voluntary behavior and leave communication with parents intact. No doors in communication between parent and child are closed with consistent enforcement of parental expectations.**

Useful rules are difficult to formulate. They represent things parents really believe the child will eventually do voluntarily. Consequently, parents must be able to believe in their children. This takes faith—belief without evidence—because the very nature of believing something that is not now in evidence, and may not be in evidence for a long time, requires faith. Rules represent the faith parents have in their children.

A beneficial rule must also be something parents are willing and able to be around to enforce. A rule like, "Don't watch TV while I'm gone," isn't helpful.

A rule must state what is expected in terms that are objective in order to be enforceable. Rules so complicated that they require interpretation by a panel of judges cause unnecessary conflict. For example, "Clean your room by noon every Saturday" sets a clear objective chore and time, but leaves open how a "clean room" is to be judged.

Such rules always lead in the direction of control because the parent is the sole arbiter of when the room is clean. This sets parents and children up for an argument. A cleaning or straightening rule must include a list of criteria for judging when the room is cleaned or straightened.

For example, the rule is: "You will clean your room every week before noon on Saturday. The room will be clean when:
1. your bed sheets are removed and put in the laundry basket;
2. your bed is made with clean sheets, hospital style (I'll show you), and blanket and bedspread on bed with no wrinkles;
3. all of your toys are in the toy box except those you are using in an incomplete game on your worktable; and
4. all of your dirty clothes are put in laundry basket. Nothing dirty can be left in the closet or elsewhere in your room."

Effective rule enforcers do not need to be hurtful to the child.

This is where push comes to shove. If you think of rules as controllers, you will say, "What? How will the child learn if there is no negative consequence?" The answer is, "Learn what?"

If parents want the child to learn obedience to their wishes, then disobedience should be punished and/or obedience should be rewarded. It doesn't matter what these rules are. All the troubles associated with trying to take charge of another human being's self-determination will be present. Teaching obedience works best if the rules are arbitrary and changing and unreasonable. Military training necessarily teaches soldiers not to question their superiors or to think, just react. That is control. If that is what parents want, they needn't bother too much about rules other than stating them.

If parents want their children to learn what they are capable of and where their behavior is headed, then punishment will not help. Persistence in parents' expectations of their children's behaviors is required.

An excellent rule enforcer is to simply say in a calm even voice, "The rule is..."

This process is no different than teaching children to ride a bike, hit a ball, write their names, or help in the garden. When children fall off their bikes, they are not punished. Instead, parents encourage them to get back on the bike, which reassures children that their parents definitely believe they will learn to ride. Parents use encouragement as many times as necessary. This is called expectation enforcement. It would be rule enforcement—that is, an unbreakable expectation—if it were important for children to ride bikes and parents really believed the child would eventually learn to ride the bike. In this case, if the child wanted to give up, parents could say, "The rule is that you will learn to ride your bike." Because most parents don't care that much about whether their children ever learn to ride, they don't treat learning to ride a bike as a rule.

If a teenage child refuses to go to school, parents will want to have a rule that says, "You must go to school and stay there until the end of every school day." Enforcement might go like this.

It's seven-thirty in the morning and Ruth isn't ready for school. Her father stands at her door and says, "You must go to school." Ruth may say something, throw something, say nothing—it doesn't matter. All that matters is whether she gets ready to leave. If she doesn't get ready, her father continues to stand at her door and say, "The rule is you must go to school." (She has "fallen off her bike.")

It's highly likely in this situation that the father will have to stay at Ruth's door for a long time. Maybe he will need to miss an appointment or even miss work. When the rule was made in the first place, her father was deciding that he would stay with Ruth if necessary. It was also likely that Ruth would pick a day to refuse going to school that would be very awkward for her father if he had to stay with her. Eventually—probably after a giant, loud, perhaps destructive, and perhaps profane temper tantrum—Ruth will become calm and ask her father to take her to school. He will have done nothing the whole time except stand outside her doorway and repeat the rule. He did not respond to any provocation; he did not answer any of her attacks ("What are you, a robot?"). This is an example of a useful rule, consistently enforced.

If Ruth had grown up with rule enforcement similar to this example she probably wouldn't have created the situation in the first place. It is never too late to start altering approaches, even if it produces a blowup the first time. It is never too late to threaten less and to become more persistent and consistent in enforcing a few rules.

Once several parental rules are established as unchanging expectations, parents become a more believable source of information for children. Communication is possible because words aren't used to control the child. The child can understand the parents' comment, "Your grades will not get you into the school you want to go to," as information. It is not launching an attempt to make children study. This results in the child's actually thinking about what to do, and often talking over what to do with a parent.

When rules are used to control, and then thrown away in favor of more punishing consequences when they don't work, children increasingly listen to their parents for signals of control instead of for information. They become experts at complying with the rules and hiding their own secret areas of self-determination. Or they avoid their parents as much as possible. Often they do both. They will go elsewhere to learn what to expect of themselves, to friends, gangs, TV, and music. These are common sources of information concerning how people of their age behave, talk, and believe.

These are not good influences for obvious reasons. Except for friends, these sources care nothing for the children they influence. And friends know as little as any child does.

Exercise 2-A: Practice with Rules as Persistent Expectations

It is important that you not try to solve big problems with rules. Big problems—like serious and hurtful fighting among children, alcohol and drug use, serious law violations—require problem solving, establishment of communication, commitment, and time. Where law violations are involved, it is important to let the legal process take place. Laws are not rules. They represent our collective power to protect ourselves from being endangered by others. If your child is a danger to others, action is required to reduce that danger. Your child's welfare should come second to the safety and welfare of those who are threatened.

Think of three small things that you would expect from your child. Make a useful rule for each of these. "Useful" means that you are willing and able to be present to enforce it; it is specific enough so that the child readily recognizes its completion; and it has an enforcement that you are able and willing to stick with.

For example, Susan's rule at the beginning of the chapter that John mow the lawn on Friday when she isn't at home is not a good rule. Susan would need to be home on Fridays and she would need to list what she meant by a completely mowed lawn. Does that include taking care of the clippings? How much trimming would be involved?

Tasks around the house are perfect opportunities for parents to work on *with* their children in a cooperative way. There are few opportunities in modern life for parents and children to be together, working cooperatively. Susan shouldn't throw away the chance to work with John on the lawn.

Here are two examples that will help you get started.

Example 1: Rule and Enforcement

George will clean up after himself at the end of every meal. I will say, "The rule is that you clean up for yourself after eating."

Revise If Needed in Order to Make Clearer

The problem is with clean up. I should tell George, perhaps post on the refrigerator, that it means taking his dishes to the sink, rinsing them, and putting them in the dishwasher. If the dishwasher has clean dishes in it, he can leave the rinsed dishes in the sink.

Are You Committed to Being Present to Enforce the Rule?

Now that I think about it, I'm going to have to always wait to leave the table until George is finished eating. Thursday's I usually get a quick snack and leave for bowling. Maybe I can get a later start time.

Will You Be Willing to Always Reinforce in the Same Way?

I think so, although I'm going to have trouble staying calm if he tries to run out with an excuse before completing the chore. What will I do? It seems silly to think of going after him, perhaps to a ball game, and stand there and say, "The rule is..." But I guess that's what I'm signing up for.

Example 2: Rule and Enforcement

Jean will get ready for bed starting at nine every school night. I will say, "The rule is that you start to get ready for bed at nine every school night."

Revise If Needed in Order to Make Clearer

The problem is getting ready for bed. I need a list of what that means posted in her room.

1. Put toys back in toy box.

2. Take off clothes for bath and put them in hamper.

3. ...

Are You Committed to Being Present to Enforce the Rule?

Alice and I are both taking evening classes. One of us is always at home. This means that Alice and I must agree on the details of the rule and present it to Jean together.

Will You Be Willing to Always Reinforce in the Same Way?

I can see Jean having a temper tantrum if I continue to say, "The rule is..." when she wants to just finish her game. But I think I can continue to repeat the rule in the same tone of voice. At least I know now what I'm going to do. I never know what to do when Jean gets upset. I end up being angry. This seems better.

Your Example 1:

_____

_____

_____

_____

_____

_____

Rule and Enforcement:

_____

_____

_____

_____

_____

_____

Revise If Needed in Order to Make Clearer:

_____

_____

_____

_____

_____

_____

Are You Committed to Being Present to Enforce the Rule?

_____

_____

_____

_____

_____

Will You Be Willing to Always Reinforce in the Same Way?

_____

_____

_____

_____

_____

Your Example 2:

_____

_____

_____

_____

_____

Rule and Enforcement:

_____

_____

_____

_____

_____

_____

Revise If Needed in Order to Make Clearer:

_____

_____

_____

_____

_____

Are You Committed to Being Present to Enforce the Rule?

_____

_____

_____

_____

_____

Will You Be Willing to Always Reinforce in the Same Way?

_____

_____

_____

_____

_____

Your Example 3:

_____

_____

_____

_____

_____

_____

Rule and Enforcement:

_____

_____

_____

_____

_____

_____

Revise If Needed in Order to Make Clearer:

_____

_____

_____

_____

_____

_____

Are You Committed to Being Present to Enforce the Rule?

_____

_____

_____

_____

_____

_____

Will You Be Willing to Always Reinforce In the Same Way?

_____

_____

_____

_____

_____

_____

Establishing your credibility as someone who expects certain behavior from your children, and never settling for less, is important. It leads to all kinds of benefits. The most important is that it opens the door for children to think of themselves as willing participants in the family. Occasionally children encounter a teacher who will not settle for poor, sloppy, wrong, or incomplete work. Instead of punishing the child with a bad grade, the teacher keeps handing unacceptable work back and says, "I expect you to do this correctly." Children learn from the teacher that they have the ability to be successful in life. Such teachers make all the difference in children's lives.

Parents who consistently hand back unacceptable behavior to children do not need to be angry, especially if they say, "I expect you to do this correctly." Children then learn that they have the ability to behave in acceptable ways. Such parents make all the difference in children's lives.

Two common problems that parents today have in making rules include:

- Consequences for breaking a rule must stay the same every time the rule is broken in order to be effective.
- The parent must be present in order to enforce a rule when it is broken.

The second of these, being present, involves major questions concerning one's life style, values, goals, and trade-offs. Susan expects her son John to do as he's told whether she's around or not or has a relationship with him or not. As a single mother, she has something to prove. She values her success in business and independence from a controlling ex-husband. She works hard. She loves John. But she hasn't ordered her priorities consciously. She has let the demands of her job, her feelings while shopping, resentment toward controlling men, and many other things get out of her control.

Susan only has a few more years to parent John. She would do well to examine her working hours. She might find that adjusting her values and commitments—her housing, her car, and her expensive clothes—so that she would have enough time and money to be home when John is there.

Many parents, even parents living on two incomes, earn so little that providing food and shelter requires them to be gone from home. In any case parents should not make rules that they will not be home to enforce. Put more bluntly, parents should face the fact that children have a poor chance of becoming civilized human beings if other children, TV, and computer games parent them.

Every family situation is different and has its own complications. None are perfect. I've known no perfect parents, including myself. We do the best we can. But it helps to know what you would like to do ideally. An example of the ideal way of parenting is:

- Have a few useful rules.
- Be present.
- Have good communication.
- Have the credibility that transforms our faith in our children into their expectations for themselves.

The economic demands and other realities of life concerning our partners and ourselves make perfection seem far off. But we can at least regularly review what we are doing as parents and why. Do we need to belong to that organization? Do we need this adult toy? Do we really want to mortgage our futures by borrowing to buy that vehicle? Do we need to live here? What compromises are we making in parenting so that we earn the money to pay for that vacation?

These and other questions concerning values and life style have been asked by millions of people. They sometimes change their lives for the sake of their children. It is worth considering.

Practice Record for Chapter 2

One of the biggest problems parents have regarding rules is that we tend to make hundreds of them. We make a new rule every time we say something like, "Pick that up." "Don't disturb your mother." "Leave your brother alone." "Be back on time."

Obviously, we aren't prepared to carefully carry out enforcement and consistency with dozens of pronouncements. In this chapter we have seen that just making one rule requires much thought. Yet, we stick ourselves, and our children, with an avalanche of rules.

Working toward a few effective rules means the need to stop thoughtlessly making so many of them. It means learning to talk to your children a bit differently. Mostly it means carefully distinguishing between statements that are rules and statements that are requests or observations. "Pick that up," is a rule that needs to be enforced. "Would you pick that up?" or "You dropped something" are not rules. One is a request. The other is merely an observation.

It will help if you record your progress in making useful rules and reducing bad ones. Devote three or four pages in your private notebook to "Progress with Rules."

Here are two examples of the sorts of things that will be helpful for you to record.

Example 1: Caught Myself before I Made Rules

Mike went running through the house after school, just yelling like a banshee. I started to shout at him to stop it. I caught myself and thought, "What do I want here? I'd like him to calm down. I wouldn't know how to make or carry out a rule that said he must be calm or even quiet without making it absurd. What to do? I stopped what I was doing and stood in the door to the living room until he came around again. I swooped him up and said, "You seem to be happy. Tell me about what you're doing."

He giggled and we ended up having a nice talk. I'm proud of myself when I think of where this incident might have gone, with me screaming at Mike and him crying.

Example 2: Enforced the Bedtime Rule Well

Heather has been responding pretty well all week to our rule that says get ready for bed at nine. Last night she started with, "Can't I just finish this puzzle?" I repeated the rule. She threw the puzzle on the floor and said, "I hate you." I repeated the rule. She screamed, "No." I repeated the rule. She fell down on the floor and kicked and screamed. I waited until she was finished and repeated the rule. She got up and started picking up the puzzle, and by the time she was in the tub she was laughing. I wouldn't have believed a month ago that I could behave that way or that she could either.

Chapter 3
Who's in Control Here?

"Don't you need to go potty?"

Sammy looks up at his mother. He says the all-time favorite word that two-year-olds use, "No!"

Karen asks again, "Are you sure? Let's go and try."

Sammy yells, "No!!" He glares at his mother and then turns and starts to run as she takes a step toward him.

"I'm not going to chase you, Sammy. You've been such a good boy. Why don't we just go try potty?"

As Sammy turns toward her Karen immediately recognizes the expression on his face. His eyes fixed in the distance, muscles tense, breathing stopped, he's pooping his pants. Karen's strong aversion toward that dirty aspect of life explodes through her defenses. Unconsciously rolling Sammy together with her discomfort about his smelly pants, ice enters her voice.

"You little shit."

> Sammy's screaming pierces the quiet apartment as Karen advances on him angrily.
>
> The sound of a loud slap, followed by a second of silence, and then even louder screaming interrupts a conversation between a very frail woman and her very fat cat living on the floor below.
>
> Sammy and Karen are going to have a difficult life together. Why? Because they both want the same thing—control over Sammy.

All human beings want control of their own behaviors. And most human beings think they want control of other people's behaviors as well, particularly their family's behaviors. These two wants are in opposition and will cause conflict.

Parents cannot rear their children peacefully if they think they must control their children's behaviors. In order to grow into individuals, children must strive for control over themselves—self-control. Children are born to battle for self-control, autonomy, just as you feel you need to breathe. If someone puts a hand over your mouth and nose, you will struggle, as will your child. To grow into a responsible person means we *must* be responsible for what we do—our behavior must be under our control. If we try to substitute our wills for our children's wills, they will struggle to breathe the air of freedom.

Parents' anger is a natural result of the conflict with children over control of childhood behaviors.
Parents want children to learn certain behaviors, but do they really need to control their children?

The Viennese psychiatrist Sigmund Freud found that toilet training was the source of much mischief in parent-child relationships. This is true for a good reason. It bares the bones of the nature of the parent-child struggle for control over the child.

What does Karen really want from Sammy? Doesn't she want Sammy to control his body functions? Then why doesn't she allow him to exercise that control? Surely she does not want to decide for him when he goes to the bathroom for the rest of his life. Sammy's *lack of control* upsets Karen. She wants control over *his* self-control.

Parents often want to control their children's self-control, but no such control can exist. Either children control some behavior of theirs or someone else does. Control of children's self-control amounts to stamping out children's self-control.

Sammy's toilet training is only an example of the struggle for control that he will wage as he grows up. It is easy to identify the problem in the case of toilet training because it is obvious that Karen really wants Sammy to control himself. Who else can control his body functions?

At the same time, Karen can't let go of her desire to make Sammy control himself. This same contradiction of who is in charge will be a source of difficulty between them many times in the future, especially where it is not so obvious what Karen really wants.

What will happen later in school if Sammy brings home bad grades? The question, "Who else can control Sammy's school behavior?" seems more important than, "Who else can control Sammy's body functions?" Most parents want their children to control their own behavior, and grow up to be people who:

- do what's right because it's right, not because they might get caught doing something wrong;
- are good family members because they want to be, not because others will be critical of them if they aren't; and
- are happy and successful at work they love, not at work others expect.

Parents can never really control their children except by instilling perpetual fear to act on their own, or by actually breaking them, emptying them of initiative and self-determination. This leaves someone who is always waiting for orders.

Children are not that easy to "break." Often, what appears to be parental control is actually behavior the child displays (controls) that is carried out involuntarily by the child.

Parents often do not control their children's behavior, but they can make it involuntary.

Self-controlled involuntary behaviors occur when children:

- do what's right because they fear getting caught if they don't do so;
- are good family members because others would be critical of them if they weren't; and
- do the work (possibly even very successfully) that others choose for them.

And perhaps the most bitter result of all:

- these children make it appear to their parents and others that they are living a voluntary and self-determined life.

The most important lesson that controlling parents teach their children is to give the appearance that they are doing willingly what their parents chose for them to do. This has the advantage of avoiding their parents' disapproval and punishment as well as gaining their parents' and the community's approval. The disadvantage for children who learn this lesson is that most of what they do in life will feel involuntary.

> **Children as well as adults can be made to show that they love what they are doing. But they cannot make themselves feel free while doing this.**

Sally studies hard, is always home on time, and never shows disappointment when her parents tell her "No." Her mother says, "Sally has such a good attitude!"

Sally's attitude is not about doing homework or coming home at a certain hour or never being disappointed. It is about pleasing her parents. Once she does that she also hides her feeling that homework is involuntary, coming home on time is a drag, and getting a "no" from her parents usually seems arbitrary and unfair on her parents' part. Pleasing her parents also means letting them think she does these things freely—that she *wants* to do them. That *really* pleases them.

To many people, parenting means the management of their children through control. Attempts to control inevitably lead to conflict and anger. Control means heading off unwanted behaviors with the threat of aversive consequences.

Good sheepdogs are called "headers." They run to get in front the sheep and turn them around by barking and threats of biting. Controlling parents must be good headers. They must get in front of where their children wish to go. Their anger and displeasure always remains a potential threat to their children. But they need not show their anger and displeasure as their children learn to please them or comply with their wishes.

When children have learned to be controlled by their parents, they have learned how not to be bitten; that is, they have learned how not to displease their parents. Parents are not in control of these behaviors, children are. But the children feel the behaviors are involuntary. Children choose to carry out the behaviors. But they *feel* coerced.

There is an alternative approach to child management—management with consistent rules, that is, management with consistent expectations. This method is detailed extensively in chapter 2.

It is very important for parents to realize that:

- When we choose control as a child-rearing technique, we have also chosen to use anger and upset during the time we live with our children.

The opposite is also true:

- When we find ourselves angry and upset with our children, we have adopted control as a child-rearing technique.

Exercise 3-A: Recognizing Control as Your Method of Child Management

Recall an incident when you became upset and/or angry with a child. What happened? What did you expect the child to do after the incident? Why? Who was in control of what the child did? How did the child exert control? Try to write out your answers for three different anger incidents.

Here are two examples to help you.

Example 1: What Happened?

Our teenage daughter snuck out of the house after ten o'clock on a weekday night. We discovered that she was gone and started calling her friends. After two hours of agony she returned. She tried to make her behavior our fault because we're too strict. She was so sassy about it I slapped her. I didn't sleep all night, listening for noises from her room. I don't think my husband did either.

What Did You Expect the Child to Do After the Incident?

Well, we grounded her. I guess we expected her to learn a lesson and not sneak out again, although I don't know if either of us had any real confidence that she would comply.

Why?

I'm not sure why we would think she wouldn't do it again. I guess it comes down to whether she'll obey our rules. If she doesn't, we just have to punish her further.

Who Was in Control of What the Child Did?

I guess we are trying to make her do what we want her to do. That would mean we would be in control of her behavior. But she isn't doing what we want. So I guess that means *she's* in control.

How Did the Child Exert Control?

We try to make her behave according to our rules. I guess getting upset with her and tough with her is our way of trying to do this. But she's in control. How? I guess she's naturally in control of what she does. Oh, I think I see! The incident was about two things, not one. It was about who controls her and about not sneaking out. I don't see how we'll ever win control. Maybe we shouldn't try.

Example 2: What Happened?

My son hangs around after school with some boys objectionable to us. I've told him not to do so and to come straight home. I rely on my neighbor to tell me when he gets home, and she told me he didn't get home until five o'clock. When I got back, I told him he was grounded all weekend. He just said, "Yeah, right." He kind of smiled and I blew up. I grabbed him and screamed right in his face that he's going to do what I say.

What Did You Expect the Child to Do after the Incident?

I expected him to shape up. Well, maybe not expected. I was trying to *make* him shape up. I was more scared this wasn't going to work than confident that it would.

Why?

When he was little, if I got real upset with him he would soften and say, "I'm sorry, Mommy." I don't really know how to control him now.

Who Was in Control of What the Child Did?

He was. What I'm afraid of is that those punks he hangs out with will get him into trouble. I guess it's me against them for control of him.

How Did the Child Exert Control?

I can't put a leash on him. All he has to do is ignore my wishes. I can try to punish him. That used to make a difference. But it just makes things worse now. He just takes it or ignores it.

Your Example 1:

_____

_____

_____

_____

_____

_____

What Happened?

_____

_____

_____

_____

_____

_____

What Did You Expect the Child to Do After the Incident?

_____

_____

_____

_____

_____

_____

Why?

_____

_____

_____

_____

_____

Who Was in Control of What the Child Did?

_____

_____

_____

_____

_____

How Did the Child Exert Control?

_____

_____

_____

_____

_____

Your Example 2:

_____

_____

_____

_____

_____

_____

What Happened?

_____

_____

_____

_____

_____

What Did You Expect the Child to Do After the Incident?

_____

_____

_____

_____

_____

Why?

_____

_____

_____

_____

Who Was in Control of What the Child Did?

_____

_____

_____

_____

_____

_____

How Did the Child Exert Control?

_____

_____

_____

_____

_____

_____

Your Example 3:

_____

_____

_____

_____

_____

What Happened?

_____

_____

_____

_____

_____

What Did You Expect the Child to Do After the Incident?

_____

_____

_____

_____

_____

_____

Why?

_____

_____

_____

_____

_____

_____

Who Was in Control of What the Child Did?

_____

_____

_____

_____

_____

How Did the Child Exert Control?

_____

_____

_____

_____

_____

Control and anger go together. You cannot attempt to control another human being without displaying some way to make the person feel bad if they don't do what you want them to do. This means that, whether you use it or not, you must have the power to attack them. Displaying a readiness to attack is what anger is about. Raised voices, verbal threats, and aggressive body stances are among the ways parents attempt to control their children.

The best we can do, if we go the control route, is to produce children who hide why they do what they do from us. They will maintain self-control by voluntarily agreeing to what we want. But is this the same as doing what we want them to do voluntarily? No! Here are two examples.

1. Charles joins the marines voluntarily.
   - Charles is making a voluntary choice to do what he is told to do by his military superiors.
   - Charles is told by his sergeant to clean the latrine with a toothbrush. He would never volunteer to do this nasty job. He does it involuntarily.
2. You voluntarily sign a mortgage agreement to buy a house.
   - Are the making of the payments voluntary? What if you skipped them for a while? Don't you say to yourself, "I must make my mortgage payment?"
   - What if all your behaviors felt the same as paying your mortgage? If you did everything because you must do it, would you feel free?

Children may freely choose to do what their parents tell them to do. This is easy for young children who are just as tuned in to their parents' distress as the parents are to children's distress. But this doesn't make going to bed at their parents' demand seem voluntary.

Children may also shield parents from realizing they are merely complying. This keeps parents from being upset by making children appear to want to do the very things that parents want them to do. Yet, what these "good" children do merely complies with parental wishes. What the child does is done involuntarily.

These children may maintain compliance in most of their behaviors at the expense of making their lives feel involuntary. As adults, they will experience the same fate; they will feel that they have to drag themselves through life while trying to please others.

Skeptical parents may say, "What about children who are just willful? They want what they want. We need to punish children so that they see they can't just have everything they want."

It is true that young children are not naturally very compliant. Let's face it; they are not truly civilized. A child born today is not that different from a child born fifty thousand years ago. If children are left to grow up without adult influence, only influencing one another, they will learn to act as barbarians do—pillage, destroy, and kill. If our children are to grow into civilized people we must teach them what civilized behavior is.

Learning to become civilized *does* mean learning cooperation instead of battling to get what you want.

Learning to become civilized *does not* mean learning to give up self-control.

Control over oneself is something we would like children to retain in a civilized culture. When we perceive children as willful, it is not because they just can't exist without getting their way. It's because they refuse to submit to loss of control. They want control and will fight for it. But the struggle is over who will control them, not over getting what they want.

Two-year-olds who reach for everything in sight are exercising the same self-control that they did when they were in the playpen reaching for one toy after another. Trying to teach them not to touch coffee table decorations is easily mixed up with trying to teach them that parents are in charge of their touching movements; that is, they must check with their parents before touching *anything*. Parents who are not after control of their children put things they don't want touched out of reach until concepts like property and fragility and value can be taught to children.

Children learn soon enough that they can't have everything they want, assuming they don't have someone satisfying their every whim. They learn this without our having to control them. The world will teach them.

> **When children will not back off from demanding what they want, the struggle is usually about their need to keep a sense of control over themselves, not about getting the particular thing they want.**

What we see as willful children are often those who will not give up self-control. It is important to distinguish between the struggle to maintain autonomy—the ability to direct one's own behavior—and the struggle to get what one wants regardless of other people's rights.

Examples for Distinguishing the Struggle for Self-Control from the Struggle to Have One's Way

You will feel less inclined to try to control your child if you recognize that the child needs and wants self-control. If you see that you don't need to or want to substitute your will for the child's will, you can be much less inclined to become angry and attack the child.

Read the following examples and then think of two experiences you have had being angry with a child that might have been viewed in a different way.

Example 1:

We had difficulty with our eighteen-month-old child at bed-time. We had a routine set up for the same time each night, but when I picked him up to carry him to his room and put him into bed, he would scream bloody murder. I assumed that he just did not want to go to bed and was trying to stay up. A friend suggested that maybe he would like to have more control of himself when going to bed, so I might try letting him walk to his bedroom rather than carrying him.

The next night, after his bedtime routine, I asked him if he would like to walk to his bed. He stood still for a minute and I said, "Come on," and started toward his room. To my amazement he came walking along. When I reached down for his hand he held on to my finger and we walked together to his room.

Example 2:

We had difficulty with our seven-year-old obeying. She would drive me nuts when I asked her to do something. She would just stand there or simply continue what she had been doing. I would raise my voice and would end up yelling at her. One time I lost it and just went at her and started hitting her on the butt.

A friend suggested that after I ask her to do something, or ask her any question, I wait. In other words, once I put the ball in her court I should wait for the return. I tried doing this. I had to stuff a sock in it when she didn't answer for a long minute. And then, miracle of miracles, without looking at me she got up from the floor and went out to the kitchen, got the wastebasket, and started picking up the pieces of scrap paper that I had asked her to clean up. I about fell over.

I've been doing more waiting for her to respond since then, and even when she doesn't do what I ask, she eventually says something like, "I don't want to." I just ask again and wait.

Example 3:

My teenage daughter got very upset with me when I told her she couldn't wear a see-through blouse she had purchased. She screamed and called me names and threatened to leave home. Her reaction was so extreme that it startled me. I've never seen her react like that over not getting her way.

A friend suggested to me that perhaps her reaction wasn't so much about the blouse. Maybe she was more concerned about being able to control what she wore than about wearing that particular item.

I brought this up with my daughter. It started an avalanche of words. She said she had bought the blouse with her own money and didn't see what I had to do with it. She said she was so depressed and couldn't see how she could ever control her own life while she lived with me. She went on and on about feelings of wanting to please me but also feeling that I took advantage of her and treated her like a slave. I ordered her around and didn't even listen to her. It was quite an earful.

I told her what my friend had said. She thought for a minute and said, "You know, that's exactly it. I don't really care about that awful blouse. It's just that when you told me to take it back, I suddenly felt so suffocated. And like I'd never be able to breathe while I'm living with you."

Example 4:

My teenage son got poor grades. When I approached him about his report card, I told him this just had to stop. I said he needed to bring his grades up to all Bs or better before he could drive the car any more. He blew up and then I really blew up. We were accusing each other of everything in the book. I was hot. He just would not listen.

I told a friend about this incident. She suggested that maybe my son was more concerned about his newfound sense of independence when he was able to drive than about having to study more. I said, "Well good, then maybe he'll get going on his grades." My friend said, "The sense of self-control, the sense of being an individual, doesn't work like that. He's more likely not to study in order to hang on to a feeling of individuality than he is to try to buy it from you. Being a person in charge of ourselves is not something that any of us will trust to another if the other has shown that he or she will use it to try to control us. Think of how you would respond to some man who told you he'd treat you like an equal if you'd learn to cook properly. He'd probably end up with a cup of pepper in his stew just before you went out the door with the kids."

I told my son about what my friend had said. Instead of dashing off with an excuse, like he usually does, he sat down and was very quiet for a bit. Just when I was about to break the silence he said, "Let me get this straight. Your friend thinks I want control over myself, and that when you took the car away it was sort of like a setback to me." I didn't say anything. He began to talk in a livelier way. He said that my friend was incredibly right about what he planned to do. Studying to him now felt like a defeat. He didn't feel good about it. He was planning to get a job and leave school.

We talked for a long time. I told him how frightened I was for him and how I tried to control him in order to reduce my fear. I began to see that I needed to tell him my concerns about his grades and his future and turn the problem over to him. I will keep on top of noting what his grades are and help him whenever he asks, but it's up to him to do the work.

He seemed to grow right in front of my eyes. The next semester he got two Bs and three As. All of a sudden he's interested in school.

Practice Record For Chapter 3

It will be helpful if you keep track of your successes in reducing your anger in parenting. Set aside two or three pages in a private notebook and title them:

Success in Not Struggling with My Child for Control

Using the examples above, look at your interaction with your child when he or she attempts to maintain individuality through self-control. Write down the first two successes in giving your child room to maintain his or her self-control.

Chapter 4
Using Our Own Unhappiness to Control Children

Jimmy watches his mother's eyes overflow as she reads. She turns away from Jimmy, a move that means to him that he has really hurt his mother once again. His report card is making her cry. He wants to disappear, but he tried that three years ago when he was nine after he saw a movie on TV where a man could become invisible. That's when Jimmy stood in front of his mirror for hours, eyes closed, trying hard to make himself disappear. He didn't succeed.

Finally Mona focuses on him and what he dreads most of all begins.

"How can you keep doing this to me? I worry about you night and day and now I find out that you've been lying to me about your schoolwork."

His mother's voice rises and the words come faster. Jimmy begins to cry.

"After all I do for you, I would think you *would* cry, you little ingrate. Your father doesn't care enough about you to even see you once a year. I work and sacrifice and have no life of my own, just to take care of you. Then you lie to me? And you don't even bother to study or do your homework?" Mona is almost yelling.

Jimmy wants his mother to stop talking. He doesn't know quite why except he gets an awful feeling when his mother is this unhappy. It becomes a hundred times worse when she talks like this.

Mona stops shouting as Jimmy's crying becomes louder. She pauses for a minute, waiting with grim satisfaction for his hurt to last just a bit longer. Then she starts to feel sorry for him and says, "Oh, Jimmy. It's okay. You're a big boy now. Come here and hug me."

As she wipes tears from his face she says, "You're all I have. You mean everything to me. We can get through anything. But you've got to do better in school. Much better. Do you think you can do that?"

Jimmy nods.

Anger is about control. Its goal is to make someone feel bad when they don't do what you want them to do. So any way of making someone feel bad can become a tool of anger and control. A handy way to make our loved ones feel bad, including children, is to demonstrate that they hurt us.

When you hurt, people who love you feel bad.

When the people who love you are the ones who are responsible for your hurt, they feel especially bad.

You can make people feel bad if you show them they are responsible for hurting you. Being and acting hurt are ways of being angry, of attempting to control those who love you. It is a natural thing for us to tell a loved one when they are hurting us. "Ouch! Stop that." We depend on the other person caring about our "ouch." It isn't control. It tells them the effect their actions have on us.

Most children love their parents in much the same way that their parents love them. They don't want anything bad to happen to their parents. They will take care of their parents as much as they can. Because children care for their parents, children hurt when parents are unhappy or upset. They want their parents to feel good. This is the basis for wanting to please parents. Children are delighted to be able to make their parents laugh and smile. As a result:

- Being upset can become a parent's tool for controlling children.
- Being prepared to be upset with any objectionable behavior of children can become a parent's job.

Mona sees her job of parenting Jimmy as correcting any wrong behavior. Her way of correcting him is to be unhappy with him. So she has made a habit of being ready to be unhappy. Her misery has been an effective control technique for his first twelve years. It will not continue to control him much longer. Not that she will lose her capacity to make him feel bad. He will increasingly learn to feel bad and displease her anyway.

Mona senses that this change is about to happen, but knows no way to avoid it. Jimmy's father fled their marriage years ago. He could not continue to be responsible for so much grief in a wife he loved. Mona tried every way that she knew to be unhappy in order to bring him back, including a serious suicide attempt. At the end of their relationship, the more distress she showed because of his leaving, the more determined he was to get away.

Jimmy is also showing signs of staying away. He's more silent when he's with his mother. He doesn't come home from school right away. He spends a lot of time in his room, even though the stereo and TV are downstairs in the living room.

Mona's response to Jimmy's changing behavior is to express additional distress to him about his behavior. This will drive him further away, which will in turn result in her being more distressed. As this cycle escalates, a pall will spread over the house that is similar to the period just before her husband left.

Avoiding what's ahead requires Mona to turn her belief about what causes her misery upside down. She thinks Jimmy causes her to feel miserable. But misery is something she uses in her attempts to control him. Mona attempts to control Jimmy by making him feel bad about hurting her when he scares or displeases her. She firmly believes that her husband caused her unhappiness, and now her son is following suit. It will be very difficult for her to let go of her unhappiness. She feels as if being happy would mean giving permission to Jimmy to do whatever he pleases. It seems to her that giving up misery means taking a chance that Jimmy would leave her. In reality, the opposite is true. Letting him off her misery hook is the *only* way she has a chance of keeping Jimmy close. She must give him the chance to love her voluntarily.

Taking this chance is certainly worth it to both of them. Mona will not only lose her misery, she will gain a son who spends time with her because he *wants* to be there. And Jimmy will gain a happy parent. He will no longer carry the burden of his mother's unhappiness.

In discussing both rules and control—and now unhappiness—as anger, it becomes obvious that reducing anger in parenting involves significant personal change. You can't continue to parent as you have been and just press a magic button to produce model children.

**Change in ourselves is required
if we are going to change our children.**

There is a very large reward in stopping the use of unhappiness as a way of attempting to control our loved ones. Getting rid of unhappiness we use as anger gets rid of much of our unhappiness altogether.

When someone close to you hurts you, it's worthwhile to let him or her know it by displaying your distress. In this case unhappiness serves as communication. But most of our unhappiness, especially as parents, is meant to attack, to control, to make someone feel bad. Giving that up means freeing you from a thousand cloudy days.

You do a great thing for your children and yourself if you are happy.

**You relieve your children of the burden
of being responsible for your unhappiness.**

**You relieve yourself from the burden
of suffering that was meant to punish your children.**

You will want to keep expressing hurt as feedback—communication—in relationships with children and others. If someone is helping you move a table and your finger gets pinched, you would certainly like to say, "Ouch! Stop pushing." In the same way, if your husband or college-age child starts spending money in a way that frightens you about finances, you will certainly want to say, "You are scaring me with your spending. We need to talk."

The use of distress to *control* children is what you may wish to give up. Practice distinguishing between communication of distress and distress as a method for control by doing the following exercise.

Exercise 4-A: Recognizing the Difference between *Distress That Is Communication* and *Distress That Is Control*

The ultimate expression of angry distress is the suicide of a physically healthy person. Look at the result. The person is gone. The family, friends, acquaintances, and perhaps those in a close relationship are left to suffer. Many of them will carry the hurt they experience for life. This is why suicide is the marker for the ultimate in anger and at the bottom of the anger chain. (See chapter 1.)

In looking at your own distress and unhappiness as a parent, you might use as a marker any feeling that you wish the child to suffer. Like the classic suicidal thought, "Then they'll be sorry," Mona's torturing of Jimmy was only satisfactory when she saw him in pain. Her distress lifted and was replaced by loving concern when Jimmy sobbed uncontrollably, when he was sorrowful.

> **Wanting the child to hurt is your cue that you are using distress instead of just communicating it. Communication, saying "ouch," doesn't require the other person to feel hurt.**

Recount three incidents where a child upset you. See if you wanted to make the child suffer by recognizing how upset you were. Try to estimate how much less distress you would have gone through if you had only let the child know she or he had done something that distressed you.

These two examples will get you started.

Example 1: What Happened?
Penny was still not home at one o'clock on a Saturday night. Her curfew was 11:30. My wife and I were scared out of our wits.

We called her friends' houses and woke their parents up. No one had a clue. Finally, Penny came driving in at 1:15. I was very angry and her mother was crying. We emphasized how scared she had made us. We brought up a neighbor who had been a friend of hers and was killed in an auto accident. I kept yelling and her mother kept crying until Penny finally started crying too.

Did You Feel You Wanted Your Child to Hurt?

I think so. I wanted her to feel bad. I kept it up until she cried. Now I remember why I brought up her friend who died. I knew it would get to her.

How Much Suffering Would Have Been Saved if You Just Communicated Distress?

It would have saved most of a painful night if we had told Penny how worried we were and what we did to try and find her. We could all have gone to sleep and then talked about what happened in the morning when everyone was calm.

Example 2:

What Happened?

Joe, my three-year-old, suddenly ran away from me as we were coming out of the mall. He was laughing and ran right across the street into the parking lot. I caught him, thankfully before anything bad happened. I was crying and saying to him, "Don't you ever do that again!" He still tried to laugh, as if it had been a game. I kept telling him how scared I was and how he could have been killed. He stopped laughing. And then I really lit into him with how frightened he had made me, how I would have felt if I had had to pick his dead and bleeding body up off the street. He started bawling.

Did You Feel You Wanted Your Child to Hurt?

Definitely. I wasn't going to stop until he felt as bad as I did.

How Much Suffering Would Have Been Saved if You Just Communicated Distress?

The whole thing after he stopped laughing. I would have calmed down much faster. It's a wonder I didn't get in an accident driving home. I don't see what good it did. I can't trust him to stay out of traffic anyway. I just have to hold on to him better.

Your Example 1:

_____

_____

_____

_____

_____

_____

What Happened?

_____

_____

_____

_____

_____

Did You Feel You Wanted Your Child to Hurt?

_____

_____

_____

_____

_____

_____

How Much Suffering Would Have Been Saved if You Just Communicated Distress?

_____

_____

_____

_____

_____

_____

Your Example 2:

_____

_____

_____

_____

_____

What Happened?

_____

_____

_____

_____

_____

Did You Feel You Wanted Your Child to Hurt?

_____

_____

_____

_____

_____

How Much Suffering Would Have Been Saved if You Just Communicated Distress?

_____

_____

_____

_____

_____

_____

Your Example 3:

_____

_____

_____

_____

_____

What Happened?

_____

_____

_____

_____

_____

Did You Feel You Wanted Your Child to Hurt?

_____

_____

_____

_____

_____

How Much Suffering Would Have Been Saved if You Just Communicated Distress?

_____

_____

_____

_____

_____

_____

Parents can find themselves being the "happiness police." Without realizing it, they can become the guardians of seriousness. Perhaps you've seen this happen to friends. Someone you've known growing up was as much a prankster and good-time Charlie as anyone of your acquaintances. You haven't seen the person for a while and perhaps there is a chance to become reacquainted.

You may try to joke and play in the way you used to do when the two of you were children. Your joke attempts are met with a serious or even offended response. Your friend wants to talk about the dangerous changes that are taking place in communities and families. Maybe he turns the conversation to the dangerous state of the world, particularly the misbehaviors of children and their lack of discipline. You ask yourself, "Can this be the person I knew? The kid who didn't do his homework? The kid who skipped school with me? The kid who made up off-color names for our teachers? Doesn't he remember what _he_ was like?"

This "childhood amnesia" results from your friend's assumption that being a parent is serious business—meaning that being a parent _requires_ being serious, stern, and solemn.

Some parents learn to carry a bucket of mud, always ready to throw at their children's futures if the children show signs of moving in a direction they disapprove of. The mud in the bucket is actually anger. It is refilled by talking to others about the negative state of children in general.

Some say, "Misery loves company." Misery as an attack on children finds company in the willingness of every generation to view the next as having gone to the dogs. In the schoolteachers' lunchroom, the halls of Congress, city hall, or the local barbershop, people who love to be depressed about children today can always be found. You can go to lunch feeling perfectly happy, but after the discussion turns to children today you will go back to work depressed.

The willingness to be blue about a whole generation of children is symptomatic of a lack of respect for the individuality of each young person. The opposite attitude is faith and confidence about our children's futures. None of us knows the future. To live is to constantly step into the unknown. To step into the future with faith in the way things will be is just as easy, or hard, as stepping into the future with fear and trepidation. Let's recognize that the tendency to attack your children when they move in a direction you don't like is spurred on by the mud that you and your friends throw at the new generation.

Talking with others about the supposedly nasty, worthless, and valueless children today fuels your fears and your attacks on your own children. If you are convinced that these comments are true, you will go after your children with the news that they are going to be nasty, worthless losers.

We see this same trashing of the younger generation's ways in the literature of every generation going back at least to the Greeks. In 399 BC the Greek city-state, Athens, put Socrates to death because they thought he was responsible for the impiety of the younger generation.

We are not advocating that you ignore unacceptable behavior. If your child skips school, deal with it head-on. But handle it without trying to communicate to your child that your life and the child's life are in danger of being ruined by having the child turn out like them—as if a child were a soufflé in danger of falling. Deal with the child's problems for what they are, not as signs of a forthcoming life as "one of them."

To avoid parenting anger, you must let go of your goal of control. Instead, you can influence children's behaviors by establishing credibility as someone who expects the best of them. This does not mean ignoring unacceptable behaviors; but it does mean not trying to make the child subject to your anger. If you soak up community views that "children are going to hell in a handbasket," you will be constantly fearful about your own children, or perhaps worse, falsely proud of their purity.

When your children misbehave, you can take the attitude that:

This means children are on their way to degradation and should be told that you are frightened and distressed that they are headed there.
or
This means that children are on their way to being good people, but they need to be reminded you believe that is where they are eventually headed, regardless of any misbehavior.

Punishing children with your fear and unhappiness about where they are headed sets up a choice of letting your unhappiness rule them so they become "good," or asserting their own self-rule by being the bad person you forecast.

Becoming the bad person that parents, teachers, and neighbors forecast is much more attractive to children than you might think. To become a person means to become an individual, distinct and recognizable as different from others. This is a main goal of growing up and of living one's life. When adults offer children the opportunity to become distinct by being bad, there are powerful developmental forces that pull them in the direction of "sinful" individuality and away from nameless, faceless "goodness."

This is especially true if children have not yet developed any talents that distinguish them in their own eyes and the eyes of adults. The choice can be seen by children to be between being something bad and being nothing—not being distinguishable at all.

The desirable alternative to negative, fearful reactions to children's misbehaviors is communication to the child that you expect different behavior and that you will continue to expect it because the child will eventually achieve responsible adulthood. It will help you to believe in your children if you stay away from fearmongering about children in general. Emphasizing the positive in schools, churches, and community centers may not be newsworthy, but it feels good and gives you the strength to approach your children with positive expectations.

It needs to be repeated that approaching children with positive expectations *does not mean* excusing or in any way ignoring their unacceptable behaviors. In fact, it makes the thorough examination and, where possible, correction of misbehaviors more likely to happen because it is more pleasant for you. Trying to frighten children frightens you. Expecting your children to make amends where they can and encouraging them to believe in themselves is more inviting. You will not want to ignore signs that they are in trouble. Your job as a parent becomes expecting change, not communicating worry. Instead of being frightened by and ready to attack deviance in your children, you will be hopeful and ready to show them that you expect the best of them, even if they exhibit their worst.

Exercise 4-B: Identifying Ways to Become Happier with Your Children

---

Try to think of two fears you have about how your children will grow up. Are these fears well-grounded, or are they just things that you hear as criticisms of "those children growing up today."

An example will help you get started:

Example 1: What Is Your Fear for Your Child?

I guess that it really makes me sweat when my children show disrespect for adults. It's embarrassing, so I guess this fits ideas about the way children ought to be and the "no-good" children today. I feel as if they are demonstrating to the public that they fit into the category of good for nothing.

How Might You Change Your Attitude?

When I think about it, I really do expect they will eventually be more respectful. This will be a big change for me, from worry to just telling them what I expect. I don't have to attack them. I can just say, "I expect you to treat people with more respect as you grow up. This is the way you might have responded." I could even tell them that I will help them by always pointing out when they disrespect someone and that I will expect them to change. I can feel the fear leaving and I feel a lot better toward my children. I don't have to be unhappy with them about it.

Your Example 1:

_____

_____

_____

_____

_____

_____

What Is Your Fear for Your Child?

_____

_____

_____

_____

_____

_____

How Might You Change Your Attitude?

_____

_____

_____

_____

_____

Your Example 2:

_____

_____

_____

_____

_____

What Is Your Fear for Your Child?

_____

_____

_____

_____

_____

How Might You Change Your Attitude?

_____

_____

_____

_____

_____

_____

One of the best things you can do for your children is to be happy. Think back to your own childhood. Were your parents happy? If so, wasn't that a great source of strength for you? If not, wasn't that a great source of distress?

The place to start showing your children that you are happy is not to allow their behavior to distress you. Show them that just because they need parenting (after all, they are going to make mistakes, act badly, and so on) doesn't mean that they will or can make your life unhappy. That is why they need parents, because they are not yet responsible adults. *But they will be.*

Making the changes recommended here would require life changes for most people. No one, except perhaps some saints, could be happy and have faith in their children at all times. We are placing a signpost that says, "Improvement lies in this direction." Do not put yourself in the position that imperfection as a parent makes you a failure. Any improvement in your everyday happiness with your children will repay you for having made the effort.

Keeping track of change helps us change. You will benefit from setting aside four or five pages in your private notebook for recording successes in changing your attitude toward your children from one of fear of their failures to hopeful expectations and communication of those expectations. You need not become miserable in order to parent effectively.

Here is an example of how you might set up your notebook for keeping track of successes.

Practice Record For Chapter 4

Example of Becoming More Happy as a Parent

Last night I went to pick up Ron from his junior play practice. It was supposed to be over at 9:00. I waited until 9:15 and no Ron. I went into the building and only the janitor was there. He said that practice let out early. I was frightened and angry. I didn't know what else to do, so I went home intending to call around to Ron's friends. He was there when I got home.

He said, "We got out early and Sue gave me a ride. I thought I'd make it before you left."

I felt a choice looming before me. I wanted to let him have it and make him feel my fear when I did not find him at school. I said to myself, "There is another way." To Ron I said, "When you make arrangements for me to pick you up, I expect you to be there just as you would expect me to be there."

He said, "I didn't think about it like that, Mom. Sorry."

I had a good evening.

Chapter 5
Withholding Family Inclusion as a Parental Anger Tool

Philip maneuvers his bike expertly off the sidewalk and through the sandy corner park to save time. His featherweight mountain bike flies easily up the small bank on the far side. Popping out of the park and soaring into the air, he clears the sidewalk and curb on the street near his house. Now on the home stretch, he spots his father's car already in the driveway. He stops pedaling and the forbidden expletive, "Shit!" bursts out like the crack of a small caliber rifle.

"Phil, where are you?" rings out from the open front windows as Philip pulls into the drive.

"I'm out here." He carefully puts his most valued possession up on hooks in the garage. "I'm coming."

> Philip, head down, opens the door from the garage to the kitchen, and drags his body through to face the music.
>
> "I don't know who you are these days, Phil," his father says. "You agreed that you would take charge of cleaning and maintaining the pool if we got you that bike on your twelfth birthday. We used to be able to trust what you said. What's going on? Are you on drugs or something? And look at me when I talk to you!"
>
> Phil raises his head, forcing his eyes to follow. "I'm *not* on drugs," he manages to say. Then his body seems to collect itself to form a taller young man. "Is that what you think of me?"
>
> "I don't know what to think of you. You seem lost, as if you're somewhere else a lot of the time. You don't seem happy around the house. You don't do your chores. What should I think? You tell me."

There are two very different possibilities for what is going on at this time in Philip's life. One is unavoidable in our culture because we start adulthood later than biology initiates it.

Philip is entering puberty. His body is changing rapidly. This metamorphosis is biology's way of forming an adult body. In many cultures in the history of humankind, Philip's community would be reviewing what he had learned and readying him for the ceremonies necessary for welcoming him into its full membership as an adult. But Philip's family, school, and community are not even close to recognizing Philip as being either a biological adult or an adult member of the community. This is a normal, but treacherous, time for all families.

We must be welcomed into a community in order to identify who we are. Who we are, our identities, are formed from our relationships. In order to identify himself as a real person, Philip must have full membership in the community of real people. Philip's membership status is unclear to him, and this confuses Philip about who or what he is.

Why is Philip unclear about who he is?

The answer is connected to parental patterns of control and anger and is much more serious for all concerned than children becoming confused about when they are adults.

In order to learn what it feels like to be an adult, children must at some time be related to as if they *are* adults, *by* adults. This treatment tells children they are like those adults.

"People like me" is the basis of identifying who one is. These people react to children's welfare in the same way they react to their own welfare and expect the same from children. This is one's moral community, moral because treating others in the way one treats oneself reveals an ethical attitude.

Unfortunately, given the history of humankind and present practice, moral communities do not (yet) include all people. People seen to be outside one's moral community are not treated in the same way as insiders. They are not viewed as real people. Their hurts are not seen to be the same as those of insiders. They are different and not to be thought about except as candidates for charity, and only then if they aren't too demanding.

Children must be welcomed into the moral community, the community of "people like us," or they will not know who they are or how to behave, and they will feel they are not real people.

Perhaps you, as an adult, have not always experienced yourself as an adult. "I still don't know what I want to be when I grow up," is an adult joke, but a revealing one. "I don't feel grown up," is a common complaint of some adults. Feeling like a full-fledged member of the socially interdependent human community will only occur if one is invited into the community and full membership is conferred. If this did not happen when you were a child, others will easily manipulate your feelings of belonging and rejection when you are a teen or an adult. The awful feeling of being on the outside will be lurking, ready to emerge, if others ignore or reject you.

Feeling outside the moral community is painful.

Parents and other authorities can easily use this painful outside experience to punish and control children. Banishment is an age-old punishment used in many cultures. Threat of banishment is the tool that can be used for control.

"If you keep it up, you will be just like those losers." Translated into "child emotional talk," this means, "You may be a person who doesn't belong." Billions of dollars are spent by teens to ward off the potential pain of not belonging. Adults spend many more billions in order to try to validate their membership in the community of those who matter to them.

Parents who use threats and anger to control children find it easy to threaten exclusion from our community to punish children. Philip's father said, "I don't know who you are." This is only his most recent version of an alienating theme that goes back a long way in Philip's life. Philip feels a terrible fear when he hears his father talk like this. His fear is that his father is questioning if he is really one of them. His longstanding dread is that "I don't belong. I am one of those whom my parents reject." This practice forms the basis for exclusionary practices by the culture such as prejudice.

Families that practice prejudice toward any group of others run the risk of disowning their own children. It is handy for parents to attack their children when they misbehave with the charge that the children will grown up to be "like those others."

Philip is used to hearing his parents disparage others, a wide variety of others. Lazy welfare bums, unethical Jews, demanding blacks, lazy neighbors with untrimmed yards, and women who have careers and neglect their children are all equally unworthy human beings in his parents' minds. All these and more have been the targets of snide remarks and occasional critical dissertations from Philip's parents. Philip has no question that his parents exempt these groups from their expressions of ordinary sympathy and kindness, which they show even to a lost puppy. Outsiders deserve anything that happens to them, and the last thing anyone should do is to help them.

Philip's parents' angry attitudes were not lost on him as he grew up. It seems to him that sometimes his parents take for granted that he is a legitimate human being, just as they are. At other times they make it clear that he is nowhere near being someone they would gladly call their own.

**Philip's welcome into his parents' moral community,
the community of people they will treat like themselves,
is never fully given to him or felt by him.**

**Philip's identity as his parents' child,
who will grow into someone like his parents,
is always tentative.**

Knowing who we are and belonging are two sides of the same coin. If Philip never knows for sure whether he belongs to the community he's being reared in, even at the level of his family, then he also never knows for sure who he is. He will soon become painfully aware that his parents use keeping him on probation in order to control him.

It's like being asked to join a club, but never getting past probationary status, because there is always something more to do for the club to prove you really belong there. When Philip's parents are upset with him, they give him something more to do in order to prove he deserves their welcome into the community of selves who belong.

And there *is* always something more if what is required is always doing what Philip's parents want him to do. To effectively control him, Philip must always remain on probation. To grant him full membership in their community would be to relinquish this tool of control.

Exercise 5-A: Using Exclusion to Show Anger toward Your Children

Fear is the common motivator for parents who threaten their children with not belonging. Fear that turns into anger is a good clue to look for when you try to find out if you use exclusion to threaten your children to control them.

Philip came home late and hadn't done a chore he promised to do. This awakened one of his father's fears about his children. The father is highly judgmental of "worthless people." He sees his job of parenting as being vigilant for any deviance. Like a parent who believes illness lurks everywhere, threatening to make children sick, Philip's father believes children who grow up into worthless people are everywhere. "Maybe Philip is really like one of those people I think are worthless."

The father then turns his fear into an attack on Philip, which takes the form of "I don't know who you are." This means, "I don't know you as a member of this family."

Parental accusations such as "You're a lazy bum. I don't know how you will ever survive as an adult. You're just like those worthless...You're going to be a..." communicate that you think your child doesn't fit into your family.

Attacks in the form of comparing the child's "bad" behavior to that of another child, particularly a sibling, function as exclusions. "Your sister was getting all As at your age. Why can't you be like her? I could always depend on your brother when…" are especially exclusionary. They say, "X got in, but you didn't."

Try to remember three times when you have excluded a child. Remember, if you examine what frightens you about your child's future, you will often discover attacks that use exclusion as a weapon.

These two examples will help you get started.

Example 1: The Incident

Mike's third-grade teacher called our home one evening and told my wife that she caught Mike with a note from a girl in the class. The note asked him if he knew how they took temperatures in the hospital and asked him to meet her. Mike had scribbled okay on the note. The teacher said she thought we ought to know about this.

The Attack

I do remember being mostly embarrassed to begin with. Our older children have done very well in that school and our family is respected in the community. My embarrassment changed to anger, especially when my wife said, "You take care of it."

I didn't really know what to take care of, but what I did do was to confront Mike in his room. I asked him who this little girl was. I'm afraid I tried to give him the idea that there was something wrong with her, that she is lower class and that no one was going to respect her. And then I said, "Is that the way you want to turn out? Instead of being someone the teachers think highly of, like your brother and sister, do you want them to dismiss you as a loser?"

This really got to Mike and he broke down crying. Since then, it seems as if he's been kind of sad. He doesn't approach me when I get home. If I don't seek him out, I don't get to talk to him.

Example 2: The Incident

Sandy, our fourteen-year-old, was yelling at her little brother one evening. She was really screaming at him, accusing him of taking some money out of her room. It was so loud that I was sure that all the neighbors could hear her carrying on.

The Attack

I was afraid and embarrassed. I was afraid that the nice relationship I had always hoped my family would have would just be killed by Sandy's extreme reaction to her brother. I felt the family was about to fall apart. I was embarrassed by the thought that the neighbors were probably listening and thinking what a low-class bunch we are.

I started in on Sandy with, "What kind of a person are you? This is your brother you're screaming at. You've been parked up here in this room by yourself doing what? I don't recognize you any more. You act like some kind of creep who has no manners and no sense of what's right and wrong." She started to cry and I felt as if I'd gone too far. I tried to reach out for her, but she pulled away and shouted, "Get away from me!"

Your Example 1:

_____

_____

_____

_____

_____

_____

The Incident:

_____

_____

_____

_____

_____

_____

The Attack:

_____

_____

_____

_____

_____

_____

Your Example 2:

_____

_____

_____

_____

_____

The Incident:

_____

_____

_____

_____

_____

The Attack:

_____

_____

_____

_____

_____

Your Example 3:

_____

_____

_____

_____

_____

_____

The Incident:

_____

_____

_____

_____

_____

_____

The Attack:

_____

_____

_____

_____

_____

_____

The family is the child's first natural moral community, which, by definition, consists of those whom we treat in the same manner as we treat ourselves. By the same definition, if our family is our only moral community, we will treat those outside the family in a different way. Literally, our moral attitude, our concern and regard toward others, will not extend to those outside the family in the same way as it does to those perceived to be in our family.

We are more likely to be able to hurt and injure those whom we see as outside than those whom we see as inside our moral community. Fraternities are able to haze even prospective (probationary) members viciously. Cliques are able to inflict lifelong injurious humiliations on those unlucky souls who are found by them to be outside. "Moral people" can direct lynchings, burnings, crucifixions, and even cannibalizations without guilt toward those outside their kin, their clan, their religion, their tribe; namely, "their own kind."

> **Excluding other persons from our own moral community releases us, psychologically and morally (in our eyes), from concern for their welfare. Therefore, people who are "moral" in their interactions with their "own kind" can carry out terrible acts toward people they do not view as their own kind.**

Children who are kept on probation as members of the family's moral community are in danger of being treated in the same way as outsiders. Being on probation isn't the same as meeting disapproval from parents or others in the family. Those with solid credentials in the family can be shown disapproval by other members without threat of being put outside. It is only when the disapproval comes in the form of questioning the child's status in the family that probation, rather than full membership, is affirmed. "You are just like X. You will never be someone I can depend on. You are just bad, that's what you are."

Identifying a child as a "bad child" can mean to the parent that the child is outside the moral community. This allows the parent to hurt the child without recognizing the child's distress.

To the parent, attacking a child can be as natural as attacking "those people." If the world has many people whom you condemn—that is, if you have many prejudices—your children are likely to experience a strong fear. Your children will fear that you will use these same waste bins to discard them. When you disapprove of groups of people, your children hear the message that these people are bad. When you disapprove of your children's behavior, they will easily hear the message that they are one of "those," rather than one of "us."

The contrary is also true. If you talk inclusively about all people, your children will feel you welcome them into your moral community. They will take it for granted that they will never be on probation. If you disapprove of something they do, the disapproval does not raise the issue of rejection. Your disapproval says, "I insist that you act like this." It does not say, "You are acting like someone I reject as being unlike me."

Like it or not, we are all capable of cruelty toward others when we see them as not really being people. When we see others as objects that do not have feelings, experience love, have ambitions, have families they love, and dream dreams, it gives us "moral" permission to treat them as we would a weed in the garden. When a parent attacks a child as being unlike and unworthy of being a legitimate member of humanity, the parent is likely to feel no hesitation in mistreating the child.

Once again we face the fact that if we are to reduce the use of anger with children, we must change. It isn't just a matter of learning this or that technique or trick. We must change ourselves. Welcoming children into the family as a moral community—that is, a group of people who feel each other's pains and successes as they do their own—requires that we recognize and minimize our prejudices as much as we possibly can.

Suppose you wish to calm and win the trust of a frightened child. While you are doing this, you frequently interrupt your interchange with shouts and putdowns of other people that happen by. Do you think you could win the child's trust this way? Trying to include a child in your family as a full-fledged member while your child sees you emphasizing rejection and criticism of others and demeaning those who displease you, results in a child who does not know who he or she is, especially when you are showing displeasure.

One of the most telling areas for building your children's confidence in being a person or being on probation as a person, is your treatment of your children's friends. Making children's friends welcome as guests of the family reassures children.

> **Welcoming your children's friends as legitimate guests of the family reassures your children that they are legitimate members of the family.**

The phrase "with all its rights and privileges" is included when college degrees are granted to students. Part of being a member of a family is to have some rights and privileges of membership. Granted, the rights are different for older children than younger, different for children than parents, but there should be rights for all.

One of the most basic family rights is to choose friends who will be respected by others in the family, at least until the person shows himself or herself to be dangerous or untrustworthy. The exclusion of friends because of skin color, name, family, grades, hair appearance, or clothing says to your children that only certain kinds of people are legitimate like "us." And your children are themselves suspect for consorting with "one of them."

> **Children go where they are welcomed, and those who welcome them, at least to some extent, influence their identities.**

It has been said, "It takes a village to raise a child." We might add that this is especially true if parents don't raise them. It is true that whether or not children's families welcome them into their moral community, children will gravitate toward any group that will welcome them. Churches, athletic teams, gangs, the family down the street all offer children "moral membership" and contribute to children's identities. Even criminal groups must have some form of morals with respect to each other. Otherwise, their groups would self-destruct.

Exercise 5-B: Taking Your Children Off Probation and Keeping Their Family Membership Active

---

The bottom line is to do everything you can to welcome your children into the family and make their membership irrevocable. It is extremely important that when you become disapproving, or especially when you become angry with your children, you maintain your view of them as family members. If you start to lose this view, you will find yourself attacking your children with no sympathy for the pain your attack is producing in them.

It is particularly important to keep children feeling they are welcome family members in blended families; that is, families with children from former marriages of both parents. Parental squabbling over equal treatment of the children is not only harmful to the children, it often becomes the source of serious marital problems.

A good clue to use for detecting your children's status is the way you feel about their anticipated discomfort when you show them your disapproval. If their pain causes you discomfort, then you are viewing them as continuing to be inside your family. If you feel their pain as merely a satisfaction of your anger, then you have—at least temporarily—dumped them from membership in your family as a moral community.

Try to remember two incidents when you felt bad for your child after you disciplined him or her, but felt only anger or righteous indignation while you were carrying out the discipline.

Two examples will help you see what to look for:

Example 1: The Incident

I found a plastic bag with stems and seeds in it under our fifteen-year-old boy's mattress. I looked around and found a glass pipe with marijuana resin in the bowl stuffed back on the top shelf of his closet. When he came home I started yelling at him. I accused him of stealing because I knew he couldn't afford to buy drugs. I told him he could no longer be in contact with his friends because they were a bunch of potheads. I went on and on. He sat there with his head down almost between his knees. While this was going on I felt nothing toward him except anger and betrayal.

Your Feelings Later

It took a long time for me to change my feelings. For days I glared at him whenever he was around. I found him making his own lunch one day. I usually make it for him. I said, "Good. You'd better learn to make sandwiches. That's probably how you'll end up making a living."

I began to come to and the things I had said to him started to stab me like knives. I realize now that I had done nothing to solve the problem except practically disowning him.

What Could You Have Done?

I see now that I didn't even know what he had done, who he was doing it with, what he thought about it, or anything. And now we had zero communication. I could have decided to talk to him about my lack of knowledge about what was happening and ask him to help me out. I could have suggested that he invite his friends over and have a meeting where they shared what their concerns and beliefs were about drugs. I could have promised to contribute nothing except questions and food. This feels much more solid. Maybe it's not too late.

Example 2: The Incident

Ruth came home from high school with a new friend. This friend was wearing jeans with holes all over, patched with different kinds of material, including a big patch right in the crotch. She had rings all around her ears and on her eyebrows and nose. I couldn't stand to look at her. After she left, I asked Ruth in a really sarcastic voice, "What the heck was that?"

Ruth looked angry immediately and said, "She's not a 'that.' She's a human being. She's one of the coolest kids in my class if you want to know. But she probably doesn't meet your standards. Maybe I don't either."

This made me angry. I said, "Well, maybe you don't."

Your Feelings Later

I immediately felt terrible. I felt I had just thrown her out of my life.

What Could You Have Done?

That's simple. All I had to do was to let Ruth tell me about this girl. She was already excited about a new friend. The fact that she brought her home meant that she expected me to accept her.

Your Example 1:

_____

_____

_____

_____

_____

_____

The Incident:

_____
_____
_____
_____
_____
_____

Your Feelings Later:

_____
_____
_____
_____
_____

What Could You Have Done?

_____
_____
_____
_____
_____

Your Example 2:

_____
_____
_____
_____
_____

The Incident:

_____

_____

_____

_____

_____

_____

Your Feelings Later:

_____

_____

_____

_____

_____

What Could You Have Done?

_____

_____

_____

_____

_____

_____

Keeping your children off probation as family members is one of the most fundamental things you can do to influence their identities and their happiness as adults. A hundred years ago, when most people lived on farms and in rural areas, it was much easier and more natural to welcome children into their families in a way that stabilized their identities. Children hunger for chances to be like their parents.

In the past, children worked together with their parents in farm families, rejoicing when their parents gave them a chance to do a task that was more adult. Each invitation from the parent was an affirmation of the child's status and identity as a member of the family.

These opportunities are not available to most families today. But often families squander the chances that do remain to them to work with their children and offer their children the chance to help them do adult things.

Working on the lawn or landscaping or remodeling or decision-making about these things are all opportunities to work with your children. Often parents just assign their children to do certain chores and then leave them to it. This is okay to some extent. But try looking at every such assignment as an opportunity for you to work with your children. Do the yard work together. Ask your children what they think about plantings or how to accomplish some effect. Every inclusive action you make with your children confers an identity as a member of a moral community on them.

Practice Record for Chapter 5

Writing down incidents that you are proud of is a great help in making changes that really matter to you.

Make room in your private notebook for recording three or four incidents where you were able to recognize the danger signal that you were about to put your child on probation. In addition, leave room for recording at least three ideas you came up with to share decisions and tasks with your children.

Here's an example of a recorded incident that helped a child to identify as a member of the family.

Date: 12/08
Incident

My wife and I were trying to decide whether to buy and fix up a rental house. We sometimes do this if we can see a way to do some work ourselves and so increase the income potential of the property. We had gone round and round about this particular house, but we just couldn't decide.

Finally it occurred to me that we needed fresh eyes to look at the house. Our sixteen-year-old daughter had listened to most of what we talked about at home, but hadn't said a word. I said to my wife, "Let's drive Ann over there to take a look and see what she thinks."

We asked Ann, but she said she didn't know anything and so on, yet she seemed pleased to be asked. After looking around the place again with her and answering her questions, Ann said, "You know, one of my friends from school lives a couple of doors down from here. She told me she's going to have to go to South Central after this year because they're changing the district lines. South Central is a good school, but it's a long way away. She said that her parents, and a lot of others around here, are planning to move to keep their children in North Central High or to get closer to South Central."

My wife and I looked at each other and then hugged her. My wife said to her on the way to the car, "Annie, you just saved us a lot of money. How'd you like to stop for a burger?"

Chapter 6
Parental Anger and Childhood Self-Importance

"He's such an ingrate!" Jeb thunders at his wife. "We've given him everything anyone could want. And God knows it cost us plenty. Many times we didn't even have the money, but we still found a way for him to have the best clothes. Last year we got him a new car when he turned sixteen. Now I ask him to help me with the lawn and he says he's too busy.

"Then he made that crack about his friend whose father hires the lawn work done. I swear, Kathy, I almost hit him. If I hadn't turned and walked away, I think I would have. When I got in control and told him he would have to help me with the lawn, he sulked. He moved around at about the speed of a caterpillar. Finally, I got sick of him and told him to go do what he had to do. He left without saying a word."

"He's just a kid, Jeb. He'll thank us someday. Right now, he's just too young to see what we're doing for him. He expects it because we've always been there for him. Think what it was like for us growing up. Your parents didn't even let you use their car, much less buy you one. We both had to work after school to have things we wanted. And then our parents made us use our money to buy our own clothes."

"You're right, Kathy. One of my friends even had to pay rent at home. Can you imagine that today, a high-school kid paying rent to his parents?

"But Kathy, I don't know if I can stand his attitude any more. He seems to be getting snottier and snottier. He acts like he's superior to us. My father would have landed me right on my behind if I had talked to him the way Junior talks to me. I've always said that I would never treat my children the way I was treated. But I swear one of these days I'm going to slap him silly."

Jeb's prediction is likely to pan out. He is likely to lose it as Junior gets even more unpleasant, which he will.

Jeb's parents' generation would have diagnosed Junior as a spoiled child. They used to tell Jeb and Kathy that they did too much for their son. Jeb didn't listen because he thought it was mainly coming from their idea that children needed punishment, and lots of it. Jeb and Kathy wanted to use love to rear their children. They lavished a lot of care and concern on Junior, thinking that he would feel loved by them in a way they didn't feel loved while growing up.

Unfortunately, despite all he's been given, Junior doesn't feel loved, he feels self-important. He feels that he is owed everything he wants. The feeling that others, particularly his parents, owe him leads him to more angry demands. Now the more he demands, the more fed up his parents become with him.

Junior's parents thought that they could build his self-esteem and self-confidence by assuring him that he is loved. They tried to make sure that he could depend on them when in need by relieving him of any form of distress.

The result is not a child with good self-esteem. Instead, Junior expects his parents and others to keep him from distress and to deliver anything he desires. Junior's parents have a high level of anger and resentment at Junior because of his growing willingness to use them.

Angry parents of teenagers who are over the top in their demands are common. These situations can easily get out of hand. They can lead to various tough-love solutions that are essentially abandonment of children who haven't the psychological tools to survive.

Self-importance is made up of the persistent belief that others owe it to you to solve your problems. It grows from the belief that you deserved what was actually given to you.

Self-esteem is made up of the persistent belief that you can find your own solution to your problems. It grows with the belief that obstacles can be overcome.

Note that, as parents, we *are* there to solve the problems of our children when they are infants. This is natural and necessary. But by the time our children are teenagers, we are *not* there to solve their problems. We are there to solidify their membership in the community of people, "selves" if you will, that give, receive, trade for equal value, and love.

A parent's anger at self-important teenagers arises because the child acts as if the parent owes what the parent is giving out of (mistaken) love.

In order to reduce our children's self-importance, we must change our own behaviors. First, we must get over our anger at their self-important demands. Anger merely leaves self-important children feeling that they have been cheated. They *do* feel that their parents owe them. When the parents angrily attack them, they react as anyone would who is owed something. Instead of being paid, they are attacked by their debtor. In other words, they act very much as their parents are acting—angrily.

Exercise 6-A: Identifying Self-Importance and Ignoring Its Demands

It is useful to be prepared beforehand for the self-important demands of teenagers. A good way to prepare yourself is to develop a view of the child's behavior that isn't so personal. For example, imagine the self-important child as the naked king in the children's story about the king's new clothes. Self-importance is the child's new clothes. It leaves self-important people naked because they have no commanding position that justifies demands on their subjects.

Another view is to imagine your unpleasant, demanding child as a diplomat who was out of the country when his or her government changed. Upon return, the diplomat starts giving orders to others without realizing he or she no longer has any status that justifies it.

Do not use these views to belittle or mock your child. Use them only for your own relief from angry responses. What is not taken personally isn't as anger-provoking.

Try to remember three instances during which you became very angry with an older child because the child seemed ungrateful or exhibited an attitude of "you owe it to me." Then imagine going back to the instances with a more impersonal approach. Write down your attitude changes and revise them until the heat from the incidents cools down.

Two examples will help you get started.

Example 1: Incident

Harold, our fourteen-year-old, started complaining about his basketball shoes. I asked him what was wrong with them. His mother had gone with him at the beginning of the season and he picked them out. They cost over a hundred dollars. Then two weeks later he's complaining to me about them. He said they're crap and the other kids all had a different brand. I said no new sneakers, and he got very agitated and yelled that I never give him anything except the cheapest stuff. I got very angry and it escalated from there.

Imagine an Impersonal Reaction

I go through what happened in my imagination. Thinking of his cheapskate charge, I realize that's where things went off track. I'm always a little hesitant to judge kids' clothes and shoes these days because I have no idea of what's in and what's not. I can see, though, that Harold really pulled one out of his you-know-what with the cheap remark. He could easily have explained to me what he knows about shoes instead of assuming he had the right to declare what he needed to have. Ah, that's the self-importance. I was willing to talk. He wanted only to order new shoes, and assumed he had the right to do that. It *is* easy and helpful to imagine him as a petty tyrant who doesn't know he has no right to make such demands.

Is Your Anger Now Reduced When You Think of the Incident?

Very much so. I think I'll be more prepared to deal with Harold's little exercises in "the right of kings." I will need to remember not to ridicule him and to use my king thoughts to reduce my anger and make his demands more impersonal.

Try Again If Heat Is Still Present

I'm fine. In fact, I'm looking forward to interacting differently with Harold.

Example 2: Incident

Penny didn't want to baby-sit her eight-year-old brother while her mother and I went to a movie. She argued that she had better things to do, but I persisted. Then Penny said, "Why should I baby-sit him? He's your kid, not mine. Why am I the one who has to take care of him?"

I blew up. I felt she didn't have an ounce of gratitude in her body. Everyone in the family caters to her demands. Her brother leaves the living room when she has friends over. We get her everything. Yet, she pulls this, "He's not my kid."

Imagine an Impersonal Reaction

When I imagine Penny as someone who thinks she's a queen, but everyone else sees she's not, my anger turns to feelings of sorrow for her. It seems she is a lot more alone than she thinks she is. In another way, the reality of it, she has more people who love her than she knows.

Is Your Anger Now Reduced When You Think of the Incident?

Yes indeed. I must think hard now about what to do.

Try Again If Heat Is Still Present

Thinking of Penny as a "queen without portfolio" is quite enough.

Your Example 1:

_____

_____

_____

_____

_____

_____

Imagine an Impersonal Reaction:

_____

_____

_____

_____

_____

_____

Is Your Anger Now Reduced When You Think of the Incident?

_____

_____

_____

_____

_____

Try Again if Heat Is Still Present:

_____

_____

_____

_____

_____

Your Example 2:

_____

_____

_____

_____

_____

Imagine an Impersonal Reaction:

_____

_____

_____

_____

_____

_____

Is Your Anger Now Reduced When You Think of the Incident?

_____

_____

_____

_____

_____

_____

_____

Try Again if Heat Is Still Present:

_____

_____

_____

_____

_____

_____

Your Example 3:

_____

_____

_____

_____

_____

_____

Imagine an Impersonal Reaction:

_____

_____

_____

_____

_____

Is Your Anger Now Reduced When You Think of the Incident?

_____

_____

_____

_____

_____

Try Again if Heat Is Still Present:

_____

_____

_____

_____

_____

_____

> **You will find it helpful in dealing with teenage self-important children to _stop servicing your teenage children's wants as if they were needs._ You may need to examine your own views on needs in order to get your treatment of a teenager clear.**

Do you mix your own wants and needs? Is it a catastrophe for you if you can't afford the house you want or the automobile you want? Are these the same as not having *any house* or *any means of transportation*? Do you tell your wife that men *need* sex? Is it a catastrophe for you if she doesn't comply with your "need"?

Closer to home, do your child's low grades, lack of success in sports, poor reputation, or questionable college admission cause a catastrophe for you? Are these things on the same level of importance as your child's health, family relationships, and long-term friendships?

If you confuse your wants with your needs, then you will confuse your children's wants with their needs. The pain you feel when your children are unhappy because they don't have the latest designer jeans will be the same pain you feel when you see them suffering from an injury or illness. Yet when your children exhibit demands instead of tears, you may feel used and become angry.

Your anger, which occurs when children take for granted that their "needs" *require you* to give them what they want, arises because of how the demands are made. Instead of crying for what they want, they come right out and demand what they want.

Try to see the issue of teenage demands in the light of needs versus wants, instead of demands versus being nice about it. Everyone is entitled to demand what is owed to them. The problem isn't the demand. It is that self-important children aren't owed what they think they are owed.

You may need to work on how you respond to your own disappointments before you are able to treat your children's disappointments in a more helpful way.

Do you cry inside for what you want?

Are you sure that what you cry for is really needed?

Exercise 6-B: Seeing the Difference between Not Getting What We Want and Not Getting What We Need

We need things that are necessary for a reasonably healthy and happy life. Those things we want are not necessary for life. They are at most things that would be nice to have.

Not getting what we need naturally lends a sense of urgency to trying to get it. If we have no food, we naturally put all our efforts into getting some food. If we aren't successful, we naturally become emotional and fearful.

Not getting what we want, say ice cream, does not necessarily extend to further efforts to get it. If we experience a sense of urgency when we don't get what we want, it is because we are mistaking what we want for what we need. When we don't make the distinction between need and want, we may get very emotional, even fearful, about not getting what we want.

Therefore, it is a bad idea to try to distinguish between what you want and what you need by noting how you feel about not getting something. You must think it through to determine whether something is needed or merely wanted.

Try to think of three things you have gotten upset about not getting that you actually only wanted, but didn't need.

An example will help get you started.

Example: What Didn't You Get That Upset You?

I was on my way back from a business trip and the last leg of my flight was cancelled by the airline. It really upset me that I didn't get home to relax and see the kids before their bedtime.

Did You Need It or Just Want It?

Obviously I didn't die from getting home late, so I guess I only wanted to get home on time. Actually, when I think about my anger with airlines, I guess it's all about want. When I think about it like that my anger cools off.

Your Example 1:

_____

_____

_____

_____

_____

_____

What Didn't You Get That Upset You?

_____

_____

_____

_____

_____

Did You Need It or Just Want It?

_____

_____

_____

_____

_____

_____

Your Example 2:

_____

_____

_____
_____
_____

What Didn't You Get That Upset You?

_____
_____
_____
_____
_____

Did You Need It or Just Want It?

_____
_____
_____
_____
_____

Your Example 3:

_____
_____
_____
_____
_____

What Didn't You Get That Upset You?

_____
_____
_____

_____

_____

_____

Did You Need It or Just Want It?

_____

_____

_____

_____

_____

Dealing with nasty and demanding behavior exhibited by your teenagers requires that:

1. **You do not attack them angrily.** Your anger will only confirm to them that you really do owe them what they want, but just don't want to pay.
2. **You are clear on the distinction between *need* and *want*.** If your children's unhappiness about not getting what they want doesn't make *you* unhappy, then you will be less likely to give them things just because they want them. You will be calm in refusing them. They in turn will lose their self-important, demanding behavior.

Parental anger and teenage self-importance are connected to the essential topic of interpersonal love. When we are self-important, we are unable to understand or feel gratitude. Because we view what is given to us as having been owed to us, we never experience a gift as being given freely. Love is the core of freely choosing to give to others. If we don't recognize what is given to us by another as being freely given, then we cannot feel or understand that they love us.

Instead, the meaning of love for self-important people is desire.

> **"I love you" translates into "I want you"**
> **or "I want what you can give me" for self-important teenagers.**

Junior, who began our chapter by precipitating an outburst from his father by exhibiting his self-importance, doesn't understand that he naturally has the capacity to give freely and to love unselfishly. He will need to be taught this.

Junior is confused about what is *given* to him and what is *owed* to him as an adolescent. Part of normal human development is to learn the role of love in human relationships. It is necessary to distinguish what is given and what is owed and what is done for selfish reasons. Because Junior doesn't understand anything except selfishness as a motivator of people's behaviors, he doesn't recognize either the gifts given to him or the gifts he gives to others.

Unfortunately, the more children or adults are told that they *shouldn't* be selfish and they *should* give freely to others, the more this requirement confirms to them that they are not capable of giving to others freely. Their view is that taking is natural to them and giving requires doing something that is contrary to their natural inclinations. Virtue becomes doing what you don't really want to do.

Junior doesn't need to learn loving as a duty. He needs his parents or other significant adults to recognize his natural inclination for unselfishness and a giving form of love.

Junior doesn't recognize his concern and all-night vigil over his sick puppy as love. He thinks his emotions were just concern over his property. His parents can help him see that this isn't true. He loved his dog.

He doesn't recognize his concern and worry over his mother's health a few years ago as love. Junior thinks it was fear of losing her. His father can point out that his reaction was the result of his loving concern for his mother and thank him for it.

Junior doesn't recognize that his emotional response to a sad love song is due to his grief over another's loss, even an imaginary other. He thinks music just does that to him. His teachers can point out to him that his sadness comes from his tender concern for others' hurts.

It is the welcome that his parents and other significant adults give him into a *moral community* that will teach Junior that many of his feelings are moral; that is, they are selfless and caring. He will learn that other members of the moral community care about and love him. He will find that saying "thank you" can be heartfelt.

Junior's later professions of love to a young woman will be expressions of tender caring for her as a whole person instead of merely a way of saying he wants her and wants what she has to offer him.

Much good can come from parents who learn to give up their anger toward their self-important children and teach them they are capable of love.

Practice Record for Chapter 6

Make room in your private notebook for recording some successes at substituting concern for your children's needs with concern for their wants. You may also wish to record a few instances where you spotted the opportunity to relate to your children's caring concern toward others and you were able to show appreciation to them for their unselfishness.

An example will help you lay out your record.

Date: 11/04

Example of Handling Julie's Self-Importance

Julie got very snippy with me about her hair. She said no one around here knows how to cut and style hair and she had to go to this hairdresser her rich friend goes to in the city. As I started to get angry at her demanding attitude and the "I'm too good to go somewhere here" message, I caught myself. I thought, "Let's just stay with the basics here. Does she need to do this or does she just want to." Clearly, her health and welfare weren't at stake. So, forget the rest of it. I began to see some humor in the way she was going on. Finally, I just smiled and said, "I'm interested in your friend. Tell me about her." She was sullen at first, but in a short time she was talking about how she felt about this girl. Julie was unsure she really knew why the girl was friendly, and she was a bit uneasy about all her talk about money. We had a good talk. I realized I could help Julie distinguish between her wants and needs.

Chapter 7
From Caring to Emotional Deception– A Slippery Slope

Joey races his tricycle across the driveway. Hitting the gully that forms the edging of the manicured drive, his tricycle front wheel wrenches to a ninety-degree angle. As the back of the trike flies up, Joey is launched, head-first, onto the lawn.

John watches his three-year-old, first with concern and then with fear, all within two seconds. He rushes to Joey's side as the boy starts to cry. After examining him carefully and finding only a scrape on his face, John's mood quickly changes from fear to anger.

"What did you think you were doing?" John yells.

As Joey continues to cry, John goes on in a loud voice, "Were you trying to break your neck? You could have hurt yourself badly.

> I'm going to take your tricycle away if you can't keep it on the drive-
> way. You scared the heck out of me."
>
> As Joey screams, John carries him into the house and to his
> room. "Now you stay in here until I tell you you can come out. And
> stop your bawling. You're not hurt."

Parents' feelings often change from concern and caring to anger
and disapproval when their children are endangered. A mother,
who is frightened when her daughter isn't home on time, verbally
attacks the daughter viciously when she finally shows up. The
father panics and even weeps when his toddler disappears at the
mall, and then yells at the child angrily when he's found.

Why does this happen?

Consider what is involved in keeping children safe as they grow
up. Infants require that we physically move them about and feed
them several times a day. Their safety and comfort are entirely in our
hands—literally "our hands." Their care is entirely under our control.

> **Caring for infants requires that we control
> their surroundings and their bodies.**

As infants develop into toddlers, they move about, first crawling,
and then walking. They do not yet know what is good for them
and what is dangerous. So we must exert even more control over
them and their environment.

The control also becomes more difficult. Children start to avoid
our attempts to control them. They resist and protest our control
attempts, which are necessary for their care and well-being.

> **Toddlers require the exertion of additional control from us because
> of their increasing mobility and their attempts to resist our control.**

Things change even more as children begin to learn language. A big change is our attempts to care for their safety and well-being through talking instead of direct physical intervention. We say "no" instead of picking them up when they are in danger of pulling over the lamp. Instead of checking their diapers, we ask them to go potty.

It is difficult to explain to a two-year-old the reasons for them to do as we ask. It is often easier to show emotions—fear, anger, and love—in order to influence their behavior than it is to patiently explain the reasons to them.

It is easy to forget that if language is to be used to impart information, it must be used carefully. It is easier to impart emotion than information to young children.

> **We attempt to care for the safety and welfare of older toddlers by using language to communicate emotions.**

As we learn to control children by raising our voices, criticizing them in an angry way, and saying things that are meant to frighten them, our communication with children is reduced and the child increasingly listens to our talk for signs of emotion rather than information.

In summary, we start out caring for our children by exercising complete control over where they are and what they are exposed to. Keeping them safe and happy seems to require more control as they grow. Our caring efforts meet active opposition from our children as they acquire language, which tends to require an increase in our controlling efforts.

> **Speaking louder, making threats, and intimidating with physical advantage come naturally in struggles for control in parents and children.**

As caring for the safety, welfare, and happiness of children meets opposition from them, a control struggle develops, involving yelling, threats, and worse. This is how caring for children can turn into verbally attacking them.

John's anger with Joey for hurting himself, a seeming paradox, means that John's way of caring for Joey has turned into eliciting fear in Joey. John does this by attacking Joey verbally. For John, as for many parents, care and concern turns into the habit of controlling by using angry and threatening language.

It is not news to most parents that they yell at their children because they love them. What they may not understand is that their verbal attacks, which they use as a way to control children, make it more difficult for them to actually talk to their children about real dangers. Once they start down the slippery slope from loving care to emotional language used to control their loved ones, language loses its information value. The biggest loss is the ability to communicate realistic fear over what they are doing or might do.

If you frighten your children with emotional language in order to control them, your emotional credibility for real dangers will be lost. Sooner or later your children will discount your emotionality altogether.

As Joey gets beyond the tricycle age he will need to avoid things that are much more dangerous than the driveway edging. John will become angry and emotional about Joey's learning to drive, his grades, smoking marijuana, having sex, and being home on time.

Joey will take for granted that when his father tells him about these dangers, his father is trying to control his life. John's loving care for his son and his desire to keep him safe will have gone off track.

Exercise 7-A: Being Emotionally Truthful with Children

Overreacting in order to get children to do what you want them to do is to tell them an emotional lie. If your children emotionally upset you to the same degree when they are about to touch something on the coffee table as they do when they are about to touch a hot stove burner, then your emotions are deceiving both you and your children. Chances are you aren't reacting to their touching something on the coffee table. You are reacting to them not doing what you tell them to do.

You may be thinking, "Of course I want them to do what I say." But stop and consider for a moment. If you use the emotion of alarm to rule your children, what will you use to tell them about things that actually *are* alarming that they need to avoid? How will they be able to tell whether you're crying wolf or there is, in fact, a dangerous wolf?

If you use alarm for control, the chances are that you use the same emotional deceptions to control yourself. Correcting this mistake is at the heart of the new cognitive therapies—stop ringing alarm bells and depression bells with your self-talk. In other words, stop deceiving yourself with your emotions.

But this discussion is about rearing children. A good approach to trying to detect and stop this practice is to see that you *are* deceiving children about how serious their behaviors are. When you are emotional with your children, learn to ask yourself, "Is this as serious as my emotionality is saying it is?"

This judgment presents a problem if you are used to gauging the seriousness of something by how intense your feelings are. Then it is particularly helpful for you to see that you may be letting your emotionality make your decisions for you and to stop doing this.

Is it really the case that because your excitement is very high both when your college team wins the championship and when you get a new job, that these two events are equally important? The key to seeing the difference is to ask, "What will this mean for those I love and value tomorrow, next week, five years from now?"

The same question is relevant for judging whether your emotions are misleading your child. "What difference will this make to my child's life in the long run?"

Try to remember three times when you got very emotional about something your child did and you communicated your emotion to the child. Was the event as serious as your emotion indicated?

Two examples will help you get started.

Example 1: The Emotional Incident

Our son backed the family car into the basketball pole in the driveway. He broke a taillight, did what turned out to be $600 worth of damage to the car, and broke the basketball pole. I did get very emotional when his mother told me about it on the phone. I was still hot when I got home. I told him he was careless like he always is. He couldn't be trusted. I was yelling at him. He said he would pay for the damage. I told him that wasn't the point. It was the careless attitude that he always has that worried me. He could never be trusted by anyone to do something carefully.

What Difference Will This Make to My Child's Life in the Long Run?

Backing into the basketball pole is an unimportant thing in the end. Being a careful driver is much more important. I need to ride with him more and see how careful he really is and see if he needs instruction. Maybe we could talk about it if I stay calm.

Was This as Serious as My Emotionality Was Indicating?

Clearly it wasn't, as I realized when I calmed down. I never thought blowing up at my son was a way of lying. I guess it really is. I was acting as if it were a criminal offense, which is far from the case. My son is usually responsible. He doesn't always put my tools back, which irritates me. But then, I don't always put them back right away either.

Example 2: The Emotional Incident

We are trying to toilet train Cathy, who just turned two. I'm so tired of changing dirty diapers I could scream. The other day, just after I had put her training pants on, she had a bowel movement. I screamed at her, "Why did you do that?" I was mad, but I must say I laid it on a bit. She started crying and I said, "You better cry. That's all you can do is cry!" By the time I had cleaned her up, I was wondering if I had really done the right thing. Now I see what I did. I led her to believe something that isn't true; that what she had done was earth-shattering. And I did this to make her feel bad and to make her change her behavior.

What Difference Will This Make to My Child's Life in the Long Run?

I imagine she will be toilet trained before she goes to college. But seriously, when she is toilet trained will just be a statistic years from now.

Was This as Serious as My Emotionality Was Indicating?

By no means. I made it out to be so serious in order to punish Cathy. But I see that I, in an important sense, lied to her. My actions and emotions told her that what she had done was horrible. That's not true.

1. The Emotional Incident:

_____

_____

_____

_____

_____

_____

What Difference Will This Make to My Child's Life in the Long Run?

_____

_____

_____

_____

_____

_____

Was This as Serious as My Emotionality Was Indicating?

_____

_____

_____

_____

_____

_____

2. The Emotional Incident:

_____

_____

_____

_____

_____

_____

What Difference Will This Make to My Child's Life in the Long Run?

_____

_____

_____

_____
_____
_____

Was This as Serious as My Emotionality Was Indicating?

_____
_____
_____
_____
_____
_____

3. The Emotional Incident:

_____
_____
_____
_____
_____
_____

What Difference Will This Make to My Child's Life in the Long Run?

_____
_____
_____
_____
_____
_____

Was This as Serious as My Emotionality Was Indicating?

_____
_____

_____

_____

_____

_____

It is important to remember that our attempts to make children feel bad by exaggerating the seriousness of their transgressions begins with a loving and caring concern for them. When we slide down the slippery slope from caring to attempts to control children by emotional storm, we ourselves tend to get lost in that storm.

Screaming at children who make a mess in an attempt to make them feel terrible so that they will not make messes draws us into a psychological place where our children's messes bother us more than ever. A vicious circle develops that makes us even more concerned and emotional with our children, who repeat these awful things—things that were made awful by our original emotional exaggerations that were meant to stop them.

"Awful things will happen to you if you continue to come home late" becomes "He's late. Something terrible is happening to him." The demons we summon to frighten our children will often visit *us* at three in the morning.

What started out to be discipline motivated by love ends up being a frightening emotional trap. The more we can get back to a conscious caring love for our children and away from conscious fears for our children, the more calm, honest, and helpful our discipline of them will be.

Joey's tricycle accident at the beginning of the chapter was a chance for John to carry out the job he has as Joey's father. Like a resident doctor answering a page, that's what he's there for. If there are no medical crises, then there is no need for resident doctors. If children don't need help, then there is no need for parents.

For John to carry on as if he's shocked that Joey needs help means John has forgotten his basic feelings—loving care for Joey. Like the doctor who is shocked and angry by being paged, John has forgotten why he's there.

> **Getting back to the basics of our caring feelings toward our children means converting our fears about the futures of our children into faith in their futures.**

Stop a moment and consider the difference between *fear of the future* and *faith in the future*. The future hasn't happened yet, so we can just as well be hopeful as fearful about what will happen. If we are headed in a bad direction and need to change, fear only distracts us from changing direction. Faith that we will change directions when circumstances change helps us to have the courage to make the change. It's the difference between, "Yes you can, yes you can," and "Oh my God, you're going to crash."

If he had remembered his loving care for Joey, John might well have simply reassured Joey about riding on the driveway. He might have told him, "You'll learn to be more careful as you get more experience. I'm glad you're not badly hurt—just some scrapes."

Exercise 7-B: Replacing Fearmongering with Caring Confidence

Most parents have concerns for their children. Look at *your* concerns about your children. Some are no doubt just that, concerns that come from the everyday facts of life. The meaning of a child's high temperature, the safety of a daughter on a college campus, the outcome of a blood test for a serious disease, are possible threats to your children's health and welfare.

Other concerns and fears are left over from emotional warnings you have used to try to get them to do what you think would be best for them. Getting into college, getting into the *right* college, doing well in a game, doing well in anything—these do not warrant fear. They might be your goals for your children. They might be your children's goals. But they are hopes for the future. Once made into fearful concerns, they will depress both you and your children instead of inspiring them to have positive views of the future.

Try to identify two fears you have for a child that might have originated in your attempts to make your child do something by fearmongering, by scaring your child about failing to do what you want.

An example will help you get started.

Example: Describe a Fear Concerning a Child

June gets almost-failing grades in junior high. I'm scared to death that she will end up dropping out and having a child by the time she's sixteen. I lose a lot of sleep over her.

Have You Ever Tried to Make Your Child Have that Same Fear?

Yes, of course. That's just it. She doesn't seem to care about what will happen if she doesn't study and drops out. She makes me want to throttle her.

Imagine Talking to Your Child about the Issue Without Trying to Raise Fear:

Okay, you want me to talk to her about hopes rather than fears. I could say, "June, I've been thinking that I don't really know how you see your future. I suspect I've been scaring you with bad things I say are going to happen to you. I don't think that's fair. I don't know any more than you about your future. I'd love to share your dreams and hopes with you and maybe tell you the confidence I have in you. I know you don't think I have confidence in you because I'm always getting on you with terrible forecasts about what will happen to you. But I'm going to stop that. It isn't good for either of us. Let's see what we can dream up."

Your Example 1:

_____

_____

_____

_____

_____

_____

Describe a Fear Concerning a Child:

_____

_____

_____

_____

_____

_____

Have You Ever Tried to Make Your Child Have that Same Fear?

_____

_____

_____

_____

_____

_____

Imagine Talking to Your Child about the Issue Without Trying to Raise Fear:

_____

_____

_____

_____

_____

_____

Your Example 2:

_____

_____

_____

_____

_____

Describe a Fear Concerning a Child:

_____

_____

_____

_____

_____

Have You Ever Tried to Make Your Child Have that Same Fear?

_____

_____

_____

_____

_____

Imagine Talking to Your Child about the Issue Without Trying to Raise Fear:

_____

_____

_____

_____

_____

_____

It is clear that in order to maintain emotional honesty with our children, we must be honest with ourselves about our fears and concerns. Exaggeration of dangers brings mistrust from our children and gut-wrenching fear to us. Change in this area brings a double win.

As we become better at keeping our emotions in perspective, they will remain in perspective in _our_ emotional lives, and our children will take into account our concerns. For example, if we talk to them more calmly about the various outcomes that people experience when they use marijuana, they can _hear_ us and consider the actual consequences that we are concerned about.

Many people wonder why a counselor—a stranger—can establish communication with teenagers when the parents who live with them sometimes can't say a word without starting a fight. A big part of the answer is that counselors don't get scared, angry, and crazy acting, no matter what teenagers reveal. If counselors show concern, amusement, or incredulity, teenagers know this is the counselor's reaction to what they are saying. The interaction stays on an honest emotional level. Parents can just as easily adopt the same way of interacting with their children.

Even better, when we calm down, we can again experience our more subtle and important feelings. Our tender feelings, the feelings that were there when we saw our children's smiles as we picked them up from school, speak softly. The amplified screaming of our fears and anger drown out the tender love that gives our lives meaning.

Practice Record for Chapter 7

Going down a calmer path requires lots of practice. As with the other changes suggested here, it is helpful to record some of our successes in making real changes.

As you begin to see that your love and concern for your children doesn't need to lead to exaggerated emotional reactions, your children will be confused at first. They expect you to be all bent out of shape. As they see a difference in you, they will also change. They will stop running away either physically or emotionally. These successes will help sustain you.

Leave three or four pages in your private notebook for this record.

Here is an example that may help you see what to change and how to record your success in becoming more emotionally honest with your children.

Date: 12/10
Success in Bringing Bobby Closer

I've been trying to stay calm with Bobby for three weeks now. When he came home late for dinner, I calmly said something like: "I'm happy to see you're safe. I need to remind you that I expect you to be home on time, so come home right from school tomorrow instead of going to your friends' house. I'll come home early and be waiting for you. I saved some dinner for you. Let's sit in the kitchen. I've been meaning to ask you about what you think of your team's prospects next year." He looked at me as if to say, "Who is this!?"

I sat at the kitchen table while Bobby set his place and heated up his dinner. He sat down. After a bit he actually started talking about the team. He went down through his teammates, one by one, telling me what he thought. He sounded like an experienced coach. I never knew he was that knowledgeable about basketball. I smiled all night, probably even in my sleep.

Chapter 8
Children's Attention, TV, and Parents' Anger

Jake calls to his five-year-old son, "Time to turn off the TV and come to dinner." Mickey starts to get up. But just then the bad dinosaur shows up with a roar. Mickey pauses to see what will happen. A few seconds later Mickey has forgotten that he was going out to the kitchen to eat dinner.

Suddenly the TV screen goes blank and his father's angry face appears in front of it in place of the monster. Simultaneously, the dinosaur's roar becomes his father's shout. Mickey freezes. Gradually he distinguishes the words, "Come to dinner."

During dinner Mickey's mother looks at him, then back to Jake and says, "His kindergarten teacher called. He's really disrupting the class." Mickey is examining the tablecloth. Jake asks, "What's going on at school, Mickey?"

Mickey picks his plate up and looks under it.

"What on earth are you doing, Mickey?"

"Look at the lines the plates make on the tablecloth," Mickey says.

Pauline, Mickey's mother, raises her voice. "For heaven's sake, put your plate down. Do you want some catsup on your meatloaf?"

Mickey replaces his plate.

His little sister asks her mother for more milk. Mickey makes a face at her.

His father yells, "Stop that. Now answer your mother."

Mickey looks puzzled and remains quiet for a few seconds. Then he picks his plate up again and looks under it.

Jake yells, "I've had enough of this. Get out of my sight. Go to your room—now!"

Mickey makes it as far as the stairs. There he spots a toy he hasn't seen in a while. He sits down and picks the toy up. Ten seconds later, he goes over to the TV and turns it on.

His parents hear the TV, and Jake jumps up saying, "I'll teach that kid something."

Pauline says, "Jake, calm down! Don't hit him."

What is this all about? Why do some children seem to their parents and teachers as if their attention is everywhere except where their parents think it should be?

Control of attention comes from two directions—changes occurring around us and behaviors in which we are engaged. Sometimes attention follows movements, sounds, or other changes made near us. A flashing light, someone entering the room, a sound that is different than usual can draw our attention.

Some of our attention is controlled by changes around us.
Some of our attention is controlled by what we are trying to do.

Sometimes our attention is directed by behaviors in which we are engaged. If we are reading a book our attention stays with the words on a page, and we change our eye direction in a regular manner that is influenced by what we gather is written on the page. If a child is playing hopscotch, attention is being regulated by many internal events that monitor body position along with the child's expectation of what must come next.

Roughly speaking, attention is controlled by things going on outside us and things going on inside us.

Pause and think for a minute about this simple conclusion. If our attention can be affected by changing events around us, as well as being guided by what we are doing, aren't there going to be conflicts? For example, if you are teeing off and someone says something, your attention to your golf swing is likely to be ruined. So we have golf manners to prevent the diversion of the golfer's attention during a shot. (There are few such manners in most other sports.)

But most things are not done in a quiet, unchanging place. We might be reading, but people are talking, the wind is blowing, and maybe there is music in the distance. Furthermore, every time we change our eye direction on the page, the whole picture on our retinas swims into a different picture (think of moving a camera during a long exposure).

Nature has solved these problems for us to some degree. When we are engaged in a task that requires us to move our attention from one thing to the next to the next, our perceptual systems tend to suppress changes going on around us. When our eyes move quickly from one position to another, our perceptual systems shut off vision, so that the blurry movement of our retinal picture is not seen. While we are trying to solve a problem, we are not apt to hear what is going on around us.

**While we are working on a task,
our surroundings are less able to demand our attention.**

Because our attention to our surroundings is suppressed while we are performing tasks, we are more able to complete tasks without being distracted along the way. We set out to pay our bills and are able to complete the task even though a bird starts to sing, a conversation is going on in the next room, or a squirrel makes noise on the roof. We stick to what we started out to do.

But we have all experienced times when we start to do something and get derailed along the way.

Exercise 8-A: Understanding Attention Distraction

Before learning what you can do about helping children stay on task, it will be helpful for you to spot what's happening when a child gets derailed from one activity to another. You are less likely to react with anger and more likely to look for other solutions to this problem if you can identify with what children are experiencing.

Try to remember two occasions where you started to do one thing and got distracted along the way. We are not referring to instances where you change your mind. Starting out to wash the car and deciding, while backing out of the garage, to go get gas instead, is not what we're talking about. In fact, if you think this mind changing is what children do when they are easily distracted, it increases the likelihood that you will become angry with them. You will treat the problem as if it's just a case of "He would rather look at impressions in the tablecloth than eat."

Try to think of occasions where you started to do one thing and unthinkingly ended up doing, or starting to do, something else.

An example may help you remember and get you started.

Example 1:
What Happened?

I went to the library with the intention of looking for a novel a friend had recommended. On my way past the new nonfiction section, I noticed a book on parenting. An hour later I was back in the car with two books on family problems. Only then did it occur to me that I had gone to the library for something else. I had to think back and reconstruct my thoughts to remember what it was.

Did You Do This Intentionally?

Once I picked up and started reading the parenting book, my interest went in that direction. Then another book caught my eye and so on. I entirely lost track of why I'd come to the library.

Your Example 1:

_____

_____

_____

_____

_____

_____

What Happened?

_____

_____

_____

_____

_____

_____

Did You Do This Intentionally?

_____

_____

_____

_____

_____

_____

Your Example 2:

_____

_____

_____

_____

_____

What Happened?

_____

_____

_____

_____

_____

Did You Do This Intentionally?

_____

_____

_____

_____

_____

Mickey, in the example that began this chapter, starts to get up from the TV and go to dinner. This simple task, moving to the kitchen, is derailed by something that caught his attention on the TV. Lines on the tablecloth distract him from eating. His sister distracts him from answering his mother. A toy distracts him from completing the trip to his room. One can imagine what he's like in a classroom.

These derailments of some children's behaviors by any stimulus that happens by are often breeding grounds for parental anger. Parents can do two important things about this problem to help children concentrate and help themselves stay away from escalating anger. These are:

1. Limit children's access to passive entertainment such as TV, computer games, and spectator activities.
2. Learn to repeat directions calmly to children and wait for their responses.

Parental anger is exactly the opposite of being helpful with attention problems, as we will see when we discuss item two above; that is, giving calm directions.

First, why should children have limited access to passive entertainment?

Pause a moment and imagine yourself to be the writer and designer of children's TV or of children's computer games. Wouldn't your first priority be to find ways to capture children's attention and keep it? "Good" programming does exactly that. And after the accumulation of three generations' worth of writing and producing experience, there are people who are exceptionally good at keeping children's attention.

Now imagine hundreds and thousands of hours of program exposure for young children, who are just learning to do a thousand things that require guiding their own attention while performing tasks. Putting away toys, learning table manners, formulating an account of what their days have been like, and even putting on clothes properly, all require some suppression of attention to events that could derail them. While trying to learn these things a few minutes at a time, children spend hours doing something that guides their attention with no effort on their part.

**Passive entertainment such as TV requires
no self-regulation of attention by children.**

**TV is expertly designed to guide
children's attention with outside cues.**

Children such as Mickey are trained several hours a day to let events in front of them guide their attention. Mickey is very good at letting his attention be guided by what's happening in front of him by the time he is five. This skill is in exact opposition to Mickey's attempts to carry out a task—any task. Even Mickey's ability to do such a simple thing as walk from one room to another and make it all the way to his goal requires that control of his attention come from him. As it is, he often does not make it even through simple tasks. He orients toward everything that he goes past, and something along the way often snares him.

Imagine that your world was completely arranged for several hours a day by a benefactor who continually monitored your boredom and anticipated what would be of interest to you. All you would need to do is ride along. You need not try to carry through on any plan or guide your attention in any way. Each day when this treatment stopped, you would be left to your own resources. Don't you think you might tend to respond to any event that came along? And, conversely, don't you think you might have some difficulty learning to govern your own attention?

You may wonder, "What about reading? Don't books guide children's attention in the same way that TV does?"

The answer is no. Reading is an active task. It requires active formation of events and information in readers' imaginations. When you remember a TV show, you remember what was on the screen. When you remember a story you read, you remember the way you imagined it. This is why reading to children is such a good preparation for their learning to read. It gets the active imagination process hooked up to books.

So the first thing parents can do to help their children learn to stick with tasks and guide their own attention long enough to finish them is to limit their TV and other passive entertainment. Even so-called "educational TV" is not helpful if it doesn't require the child to *do* anything.

The second thing parents can do is equally important; that is, learn to repeat directions to children calmly and wait for the child's response.

As parents, we all have a tendency to be in a hurry at least some of the time. Young children often take more time to process information before they respond to it than adults take. Even six- and seven-year-olds may not look as if they heard their parents or their teachers at first. If you just wait, they will often go into action and respond.

Often, when the child does not respond immediately, parents and teachers become frustrated and angry. The effect of this anger is to raise the fear level of the child. This brings into play another important aspect of our attention processes.

> **Fear and stress make it difficult to keep attention focused.**

Fear and stress cause hypervigilance, the monitoring of all surroundings for potential dangers.

Fearful people, including children, expand their attention. We become more vigilant when danger might be near. Like a nation on high alert, we use more of our energy than usual to look around for potential dangers.

This means that when parents or teachers raise their voices in order to hurry a response to a question or problem or order, children are likely to become even less able to keep their attention under their own control. Because they become more vigilant of what is going on around them, they are more likely to be distracted by other children or noises outside. Everything and everyone around them becomes a potential source of danger. Distraction makes concentrating on complying with a request or giving an answer or working out a solution to a problem more difficult for children. An even louder and more angry order from their parents is likely to follow, which sometimes freezes any response children might have been able to give.

Exercise 8-B: Developing a Patient Attitude with Children

What is the most complex machine or industrial process you can think of? A refinery that takes in crude oil and puts out gasoline and other oil products is quite complex. Mainframe computers, a nuclear submarine, even the total economy of a country are mind-boggling in their complexity. The United States, with close to 300 million people—each person making spending, employment, and saving decisions—seems to take forever to respond as a whole to changing circumstances.

A child's nervous system dwarfs the U.S. economy in its complexity. It has more than ten times more elements (nerve cells) as there are people in the U.S., and they are related in seemly haphazard ways. The economy takes months, sometimes years, to respond to inputs, such as tax cuts or price changes. Is it surprising that children might take a while to process a request that you make? What do you suppose happens if even more stimuli flood the child in the form of angry, hurry-up repetitions of the request?

You will increase your patience as well as your joy in parenting if you cultivate an appreciative attitude toward the marvelously complex events that take place in child development and learn to help children by keeping their surroundings calm while they are trying to respond to your requests.

Try to remember two times that you were involved in some very delicate or complex task and someone yelled at you or told you to hurry up. How did it affect your ability to finish the task?

An example will help you see what is wanted.

Example: A Complex Task and the Interruption

I was trying to do our income tax and I only had a couple days to get it finished. I could hear my husband pacing around waiting for me to finish so that we could go out to dinner. Right in the middle of trying to understand some complex instructions on depreciation rules my husband marched in and said in an irritated voice, "When are you going to finish that? You've been working for hours."

What Happened to Your Task Performance?

After I told him to calm down and wait, I went back to the instructions. I tried to concentrate, but I started jumping all over the instructions looking for a quick answer. I was bogged down for a half-hour before I could get back to slow, careful reading. Then I worked through the problem.

Your Example 1:

_____

_____

_____

_____

_____

_____

A Complex Task and the Interruption:

_____

_____

_____

_____

_____

_____

What Happened to Your Task Performance?

_____

_____

_____

_____

_____

_____

Your Example 2:

_____

_____

_____

_____

_____

_____

A Complex Task and the Interruption:

_____

_____

_____

_____

_____

_____

What Happened to Your Task Performance?

_____

_____

_____

_____

_____

_____

For young children, answering a question or responding to a request can be as delicate and complex as anything you might have recorded in your examples. They need your help and encouragement, not your anger and haste.

The problems that children experience in paying attention, finishing tasks, and answering questions and requests promptly are not helped by parents' impatience or anger. In addition, their ability to attend and concentrate on what they are doing is harmed by TV, especially if TV watching is a major part of their life. As with other suggestions for changes in parenting, it takes effort—and usually significant changes in parents' lives—to reduce children's TV time and acquire patience with them when they don't respond immediately. It requires finding and teaching activities to children that involve their active participation. It involves substituting patient, repeated help instead of escalating impatient demands when requests are made of children who don't respond quickly.

These changes may require making time to spend with children that you don't feel you can afford. Everyone's situation is different and we can give you no realistic advice on what you, in your circumstances, can afford to do. But in any case, it will help you to see clear goals—active children, patient and persistent parents. Even small steps toward the goal will pay off.

Success Record for Chapter 8

Recording successes, even small ones, is an excellent way to make changes that stick and are meaningful. Make room in your private journal to record five times that you were able to either calmly wait a child out or were able to substitute activities for TV watching.

You might set up your record like this example.

Date: 1/1
Success in Reducing Tommy's TV or Patiently Waiting for Him to Do What I Ask.

Tommy always used to watch TV after dinner. Last Monday I turned the TV off and asked him to help me clean up the table and the kitchen. He sat on the floor saying nothing. I waited about a minute and I said calmly, "We are going to clean up the table and the kitchen." He sat. I repeated. After about five minutes he got up and started toward the table. I showed him where to put things he cleared from the table and he was helpful. I told him I would teach him to play a card game after we were done. We played "War" for a half-hour. We have been doing this all week. It feels different, especially when he says things like, "Did Daddy used to do this?"

Chapter 9
Keeping the Imaginary Aspect of Relationships Helpful

Six-year-old Serena is afraid of ghosts. Her older brother Sean goes to some trouble to prepare a moment's entertainment by arranging a white sheet, a light, and a fan in the hall outside of Serena's room. He calmly marches into her room and says, "I have a friend out here in the hall I want you to meet."

Feeling proud and grown up because of Sean's surprising invitation, Serena follows him into the hall. The unexpected shrillness of her panicked screaming startles Sean. He instinctively rushes after her and tries to hold her and calm her. He says repeatedly, "It's not real. There's nothing to be afraid of." As her screaming turns to crying, she keeps saying, "But I saw it. It's out there."

> Sean loves his younger sister, but he also likes to play tricks on people. He sometimes assumes that because he loves Serena, whatever he does to her will be innocent and not harmful to her. Sometimes his assumption is wrong.

Just as marriages are partly imaginary (see another book in this series—*The Anger Habit in Relationships*), family relationships are partly imaginary.

By "imaginary relationship," I mean how one imagines the *relationship*, not how one imagines the other person. Relationships are defined by words like "love" or "hate." Even the most depressed parents who can feel nothing except pain usually imagine that they love their children.

All stable family relationships are partly imaginary and partly real. This is inevitable for several reasons. We rely on each other to be dependable and loving through periods when our top priorities lie elsewhere. We rely on our imaginary picture of ourselves as loving parents even when our feelings for our children are other than loving. Our imaginary views of relationships can make our real relationships more stable. They carry us through rough spots.

> **Being partly imaginary can help family relationships remain stable because it's reassuring to imagine that others love us even when they aren't showing it, but too much reliance on one's imaginary love and caring feelings can blind us to our abuse of a loved one.**

Grave difficulties arise if we rely on the fact that we love our children to assure us that we could never do anything harmful to them. Sean took it for granted that he would never hurt his sister Serena because of his view of their relationship—he is a loving older brother who protects his younger sister. He would never do anything to hurt her. Taking this view for granted allows him to do something that traumatizes her without his thinking ahead of time about its effect.

Parents are sometimes incredulous about having harmed or horribly frightened their children. "I didn't mean to" is a heartfelt cry. Parents' imaginary loving relationship can shield them from recognizing the true fear and horror their children experience when they are threatened. "How could you think I would actually abandon you? Don't you know I love you?"

Exercise 9-A: Checking for "Love-Excused" Abuse

An excellent way to check out whether our assumed loving relationship with our children is giving us permission to abuse the children is to pretend they are not our children but are merely someone else's children of whom we are fond. Would we then do what we are doing? Could we explain what we are doing to their parents?

Recall three incidents when you have disciplined your children. Imagine your children belonged to a friend rather than being members of your family. Would you have done the same thing? Would you have been comfortable explaining what you did to their parents?

You may want to use this example to get you going.

Example: Incident

Patty, our fourteen-year-old daughter, was yelling at her mother when I walked into the house. I could hear the screaming out on the sidewalk. Patty was swearing and calling her mother names because she was grounded and couldn't accept an invitation to a friend's party.

I was boiling. I just walked up to her and slapped her.

Imagine the Incident Happening with a Friend's Child

Well, I certainly would have been upset. But I guess I also would have felt some sorrow that my friend's child was so immature and ill-behaved. I would never hit someone else's child. Oh, that is the point, isn't it? If Patty were a friend's child, my wife and I would have been concerned. We would probably have sat Patty down and told her she was way out of bounds. Maybe we would even have talked to her about her temper and what was going on for her after she calmed down. I see. It's as if, because Patty is our child and we love her, it's okay to act badly toward her instead of taking the trouble to do something constructive.

Your Example 1: Incident:

_____

_____

_____

_____

_____

_____

Imagine the Incident Happening with a Friend's Child:

_____

_____

_____

_____

_____

Your Example 2: Incident:

_____

_____

_____

_____

_____

_____

Imagine the Incident Happening with a Friend's Child:

_____

_____

_____

_____

_____

_____

Your Example 3: Incident:

_____

_____

_____

_____

Imagine the Incident Happening with a Friend's Child:

_____

_____

_____

_____

_____

_____

Another difficulty sometimes arises from our imaginary views of our children. Because our children are in our thoughts and we experience warm and loving feelings toward them we are apt to think that we know them, even when we don't. Our imaginary relationship with them gives us an illusory sense of being in touch with who they are.

Our relationships need frequent refreshment that comes with real interactions. The more remote we are from actual interaction with our children, the more danger there is that we will harm them. Extensive talking or thinking about a young daughter—what she is like, why she does what she does, and what kind of person she will be when she is older—all done without interaction with her, are apt to lead you to decisions that are based on a primitive abstraction of her.

The imaginary relationship, when it is maintained remotely, can harm the real relationship, instead of helping it. Instead of your imagined love and caring toward a child helping you through stormy real interactions, the imagined emotions replace much of the real relationship and poison your real interactions with a child. This is why caring institutions sometimes carry out misguided actions in the name of children's welfare. The institutional view of a child, including a psychiatric diagnosis, is apt to be built up from talk among the professionals producing a caricature of the child that just happens to fit an available special program.

Our imaginary relationships with our children do not contain good information about our children's real problems.

Our imaginary relationships carry information about our attitudes and values.

Parents who are worried about their children's behaviors often build up a view of the children that is as remote from the reality of the child's life as an institutional view would be. These parents build a character in a sad play. The character is impersonal and distant from the parents. A daughter becomes a series of clichés. Plans to intervene become more like plots in a bad movie.

"She is irresponsible. She cares only for herself. She is a

whore. She's on her way to hell." This is not reality and the judgments do not contain information about your daughter. They contain information about your changing attitude toward your daughter—information about how you are prepared to act toward your daughter. Harsh and uncaring "interventions" are easily adopted for showing such a character "what's what." Anger and harsh treatment are natural when such characters are dealt with in B movies.

Thinking remotely about your imaginary daughter is very different from actually experiencing your relationship with her. Your real relationship allows you to talk with her, ask her questions, and observe what she does. She remains real. She remains an individual. She remains human. You are more apt to remain human also.

Exercise 9-B: Refreshing Your Imaginary Relationships with a Dose of Reality

Many parents live separately from their children due to divorce or long work hours that turn parents into visitors at home. The more remote you are, the easier it is to allow your view of your children to be determined by what others say.

> **The helpfulness of imaginary family relationships to real relationships is due to the stability that they give through rough times.**
>
> **There is no such stabilizing effect when your view of your children—that is, your relationship with them in their absence—is negative and angry.**

When just thinking about a child leads to anger, it is time to refresh your view of the child with a good dose of real interaction—relaxed play or casual conversation led by them.

Think of your children one by one. What is your view? Is there an angry component that sneaks in? If so, your imaginary relationship with this child is apt to be harmful to your actual relationship. If your real interactions with the child are mainly angry, something needs to be done about these interactions. In any case, try to build a loving view of the child. It cannot harm, and most of the time, it will help you and the relationship.

Here is an example.

Example: Success in Spending More Positive Time with Toby
Present View of Your Child

When I think of Toby, most of the time I think of how irritating he's getting to be. He is fifteen and it seems as if he always has something smart to say. We are getting bad reports from school about his behavior. He quit football. I don't feel very good about him when I think about him.

What Can You Do?

I see the point that my negative thinking about Toby doesn't do any good for him, and it just makes me feel bad. How can I change it? Well, I guess I am being influenced by stuff I hear about rather than just what I observe when we are together. Maybe I will block out some time together to do whatever we want to do. In the meantime I think I will try to build back the thoughts I used to have of him, ones that made me smile.

Your Example 1:

_____

_____

_____

_____

Present View of Your Child:

_____

_____

_____

_____

What Can You Do?

_____

_____

_____

_____

_____

_____

Your Example 2:

_____

_____

_____

_____

_____

Present View of Your Child:

_____

_____

_____

_____

_____

_____

What Can You Do?

_____

_____

_____

_____

_____

_____

The imaginary component of a family relationship is good for the relationship and us if we nurture it, and keep it loving and caring. It becomes harmful if we use it for anything other than to carry over love and caring through rough times.

One additional misuse of imaginary parenting is to assume that it imparts competence. Having loving thoughts about our children only tells us that our aim is to care for and protect them. It does not tell us how we can accomplish these aims.

**A loving view toward our children does not give us
the competence to carry out caring and protective actions.**

Thinking lovingly about a building does not give us the competence to maintain it. Loving thoughts about a painting do not give us the competence to restore it. Having loving and caring on our minds about a child does not give us the competence to rear the child.

So, given the dangers of imaginary components of relationships, what good are they?

Rearing children involves much joy and delight. It also involves real labor, sacrifice, sometimes pain, and above all, perseverance. A mental picture of your child that evokes warmth, and perhaps a smile, is a fountainhead for what is required for the hard times. Keeping that fountainhead unpolluted with anger, unclouded with worry, and sparkling with loving thoughts can help carry you through the difficulties you may encounter on the long parenting journey.

Practice Record for Chapter 9

Leave three or four pages in your private journal to record your successes in making and keeping the way you think about your children loving and caring.

You may wish to set up the record like the following.

Date: 2/14
Success in Making My Mental Picture of Laurence a Loving One

My wife was telling me about a call she got from Laurence's junior high principal. I was getting angrier by the second. Then I realized I had a picture of Laurence in my mind while this was happening. It was a picture of someone I didn't like. In my mental picture, Laurence was defiant, unpleasant, and a real loser. I caught myself and said to myself, "Laurence isn't here. There is no reason to have a picture of him as a nasty child." I then resorted to my memory of him catching a fish last summer. It made me feel a lot better and I could listen to what my wife said more calmly.

As it turned out, we spent the evening with Laurence, talking about his school behavior and what he could do about it. He decided to go and talk to the principal first thing in the morning and go on from there.

Chapter 10
Cultivating Attitudes That Help You Parent without Anger

Attitude is one of those things that we all know is important, but it is difficult to define. We recognize a surly child as someone who needs an attitude adjustment. Our employers put a lot of stock in their employees' attitudes. As the previous quotes suggest, an excellent way to change our parenting behavior is to change some of our attitudes. What are attitudes anyway?

An attitude is the position you are in when you are approaching a situation. The attitude of an airplane is literally its physical position, for example, upside-down. The attitude of a person is a readiness to approach a situation in a certain way. The surly child approaches adults ready to show them disrespect and even hostility. Employees with a good attitude are ready to approach company interests as if they were their own.

The natural attitude of parents toward their children is unselfishness. Parental unselfishness is the exemplar of all unselfishness; a readiness to give up some aspect of one's own well-being for the sake of another person's well-being.

But we do not bring just one attitude to all of parenting. The series of books on the anger habit, of which this book is part, could easily have been named *The Adversarial Attitude*; that is, another way of looking at the anger habit is as a readiness to approach most problems in life as struggles with adversaries. Parents often bring an adversarial attitude to parenting problems along with an unselfish attitude. As we have seen in previous chapters, a readiness to make our children into adversaries who resist our control can undermine any beneficial effect of an unselfish parental attitude.

It is a contradiction to treat an adversary unselfishly.
Caring and anger just do not mix well.

We have attempted to show how parents can develop alternatives to the anger habit in parenting. Another way of viewing these alternatives is: *angry parents can benefit from some attitude adjustments.*

A way of looking at the alternatives to the anger habit is to cultivate attitudes toward our children that help keep our homes calm and safe while fostering the well-being of our children. Some of these are:

- **An enlightened, loving attitude**—A readiness to help when children's welfare is in danger and a readiness to refuse children's demands based on their self-important expectations.
- **An optimistic attitude**—A readiness to persist in our expectations for our children's behaviors.
- **A civil attitude**—A readiness to believe in our children and a persistence in our expectations that their behaviors will change for the better, especially when no such evidence is apparent.
- **An enrichment attitude toward freedom**—A readiness to provide learning experiences in order to expand freedom through expanded opportunities for children instead of providing license and support for them to do as they please.

Starting with a loving attitude, because they have an unselfish attitude toward their children, many parents are uncomfortable in denying children's requests and/or demands. They either comply with most of what their children want or when driven to the wall, they become angry. The adjustment required is to include their refusal of their children's demands and unhealthy requests *as part of the expression of love.*

> **Because withholding feels like selfishness, parents tend only to deny their children what they want when parents are angry and feel the denial as a righteous punishment.**

An enlightened, loving attitude toward your children does not require you to feel angry in order to refuse them what they want or demand. An enlightened love is a readiness to care for children's welfare, not necessarily to make them feel better. Parents who love by taking care of their children's feelings are apt to raise tyrants. Eventually these parents will turn on their self-important children and treat them as adversaries. They *are* tyrants in an important sense. These children will run their parents' lives to the point where they must resist. The ensuing battle will drive out parents' loving attitude and leave guilt in its place.

The alternative is to cultivate a loving attitude that includes saying "no." It helps to see that one does not need to be angry in order to say "no." It really is part of a loving attitude to be ready to say no when the child's welfare requires that they not do something they want to do. Saying "no," and continuing to say it in a calm, even loving, manner brings us to the second attitude listed above, an optimistic attitude.

Most parents are optimistic when their children give them reason to be. The adjustment required is to cultivate optimism when their children give them *no reason*.

**Optimism is most helpful when it is least justified—
in the face of children's failures.**

Parental optimism leads them not to allow their children to trade failure for punishment. This is a situation in which children learn to "take the medicine" of punishment in exchange for not having to study or try to do better at what their parents wish. When children perform poorly or misbehave, an optimistic attitude helps parents to hold their children to the task. "I expect you to do this better, now try again." An optimistic attitude prevents you from simply punishing or judging poor performance. An optimistic attitude keeps the focus on the work or task in question. It is a readiness to return the work so that children learn to complete it properly and learn that they *can* complete it properly.

Parents with an optimistic attitude send their children a powerful message: I can learn and accomplish even when I fail at first, even when I don't see at first how I'm ever going to do it. It also sends the even more important message: My parents expect me to behave as they do, to be like them, an adult.

Another attitude listed above is a civil attitude. It probably sounds odd to include civility as an important attitude to cultivate in yourself as a parent. After all, don't you get along pretty well in civil society? Don't you respect other people's property and pretty much mind your own business? And that is just the point.

Civility needs to come home.

Most of us treat other people's (and many other living things') individualities as inviolable. We could never justify to ourselves fooling around with the distinctiveness and individuality of a friend. We wouldn't plant a tulip bulb and then try to change the color of its blossom with spray paint. It is what it is. People's individualities are holy, not to be messed with.

Cultivation of civility toward children means that parents are not only tolerant of the growth of individuality in their children, but that they view their children's individualities as achievements.

Optimistic and civil attitudes fit together well in parenting. Parents with an optimistic attitude toward their children are like good farmers. They water, fertilize, and cultivate what they have planted long before they can see any growth that would justify their trouble and expense. Children take at least twenty years to mature. Parents with a civil attitude toward their children are like explorers. They wait expectantly to see what new creation nature has produced. Like each mountain in a range, each child has his or her own majestic identity.

Together, parental optimism and parental civility keep alive the wonder and promise of a new life that parents usually feel when their children are born. Together they insure that parents would no more attack their children than they would their newborns.

Another parental attitude that is helpful in countering the anger habit is a mature attitude toward freedom. Many parents have mixed feelings about the goodness of freedom and a loving desire to have their children do the right thing. These parents often end up trying to control their children's free choices, which is of course an impossibility. Children learn quickly that when their parents say, "It's your choice," it really means that they must guess which choice their parents want them to choose. This is yet another path to anger and adversarial relationships between children and parents.

In our freedom culture—as opposed to obedience cultures such as Fascism, Communism, and cultures governed by powerful religions—we are prepared to embrace most manifestations of individual freedom. What does this do to parenting? Many people, including most teenagers, take it for granted that to be free means to be free from any constraints. This is only a half-truth. If that were all freedom meant, an astronaut, cut loose from the ship, floating in space without even the action of gravity to apply constraint, would be our ideal of freedom.

Freedom comes with increases in opportunity.

An adjusted attitude toward freedom is that it is opportunity. What good is it to be free from constraint if you cannot do anything? Parents' persistent expectation that their children attend school, dress properly, behave in a nondestructive manner, and learn as much as they can about everything they can does not violate their children's freedom. Learning *gives* freedom by providing opportunity. Getting along with others *gives* freedom as well.

> ## Freedom requires hard work.

Perhaps one of the most freedom-giving lessons that children can learn is that skills require practice. Whether it is learning to read or learning to play a musical instrument or learning algebra, time and effort must be given with little immediate reward except the promise of increased opportunity. A parental attitude that consists of the readiness to persistently expect children to expand their freedom by learning the value of practicing skills does not conflict with any other aspect of parenting.

This attitude will also naturally lead parents to monitor the effectiveness of teaching. Allowing children to be exposed to long periods of teaching that have no effect on children's skills is the last thing the parent who has an enrichment attitude toward freedom will tolerate. Children need to learn to escape from dull practice through mastering the material, not through going out the school door. Teachers who teach, situations that enrich, and materials that lead the child to master subject matters or skills are precious because they provide many open doors for children.

Cultivating optimism, civility, freedom through enrichment, and enlightened loving that puts well-being ahead of feelings is *your* opportunity to learn skills that help you parent without anger. As with any skill, practice is required. It is hoped that the materials contained in the lessons in this book will be a helpful aid to your attempts to improve the most important thing you will ever do— rear your children in a calm, happy, and nurturing home.

Records of Successful Changes

Many exercises appear in the book along with suggestions for keeping a record of successful changes. You may not have taken these very seriously. Real honest-to-goodness change requires doing something, not just reading about it. You need not start with the idea of doing every exercise and keeping every record suggested. Try one or two and then try pecking away at others.

Success Records for Chapter 10

For this lesson, handling an incident in a more productive way because of looking at it differently indicates success in attitude adjustment. For purposes of keeping a record of your successes, you might write four headings in your private notebook, leaving space for recording comments after each heading.

Note that a short description of what might constitute a success is attached to each attitude below.

1. **An Enlightened Loving Attitude: Successes in Loving by Taking Care of My Children's Well-Being Ahead of Their Feelings**—stayed in good humor while merely saying no and repeating no when necessary.

2. **Optimistic Attitude: Successes in Becoming More Optimistic and Persistent**—it felt good just to repeat a rule until children complied.

3. **Civil Attitude: Successes in Becoming More Civil and Respectful of Individuality**—felt comfortable with children's interests and was able to talk with them about what they like without trying to teach. Listened and asked questions without attempting to guide the conversation.

4. **An Enrichment Attitude toward Freedom: Successes in Becoming More Persistent in Enriching My Child's Freedom**—felt happy and comfortable while persisting in my expectation that the children complete an educational task.

Index

About the Author

Carl Semmelroth, PhD, has been in full-time private practice as a psychologist for over thirty years. He received his doctorate in psychology from the University of Michigan in 1969. After spending a year as a National Research Council Associate in Washington, D.C., he joined the psychology faculty at Cleveland State University. He received tenure in 1972 and remained Associate Professor of Psychology at CSU until 1975.

Dr. Semmelroth and his wife, Sara Semmelroth, MSW, ACSW, then moved to Michigan and formed a private mental health practice. Over the years he has also taught graduate classes in theories of psychotherapy, developmental psychology, and lifelong development for the University of Michigan and Western Michigan University.

Dr. Semmelroth has worked extensively with clients experiencing depression, anxiety, panic, and marital and post-traumatic problems. He has also worked extensively with young people hospitalized with serious psychoses.

His journal publications have been in the areas of perception, language development, mental health worker supervision, university teaching, and classroom management.

For more information, go to www.TheAngerHabit.com.